D1765847

Warwickshire County Council

			RRS

This item is to be returned or renewed before the latest date above. It may be borrowed for a further period if not in demand. **To renew your books:**

- **Phone the 24/7 Renewal Line 01926 499273 or**
- **Visit www.warwickshire.gov.uk/libraries**

Discover ● Imagine● Learn ● *with libraries*

Warwickshire
County Council

Working for Warwickshire

013496287 9

SIR MARTIN
FROBISHER

SIR MARTIN FROBISHER

Seaman, Soldier, Explorer

TALIESIN TROW

Pen & Sword
MILITARY

First published in Great Britain in 2010 by
Pen & Sword Military
An imprint of
Pen & Sword Books Ltd
47 Church Street
Barnsley
South Yorkshire
S70 2AS

ISBN 978 1 84884 232 8

A CIP catalogue record for this book is
available from the British Library

Typeset in Ehrhardt
by S L Menzies-Earl

Printed and bound in England
by CPI Books in the UK

Pen & Sword Books Ltd incorporates the imprints of
Pen & Sword Aviation, Pen & Sword Maritime,
Pen & Sword Military, Wharncliffe Local History, Pen & Sword Select,
Pen & Sword Military Classics, Leo Cooper, Remember When,
Seaforth Publishing and Frontline Publishing

For a complete list of Pen & Sword titles please contact
PEN & SWORD BOOKS LIMITED
47 Church Street, Barnsley, South Yorkshire, S70 2AS, England
E-mail: enquiries@pen-and-sword.co.uk
Website: www.pen-and-sword.co.uk

Contents

List of Plates

1. An inaccurate early map of the Arctic.
2. An imaginative illustration of a kayak.
3. A sixteenth-century astrolabe.
4. The cross staff in use by a sixteenth-century navigator.
5. A sundial and compass dating from the late sixteenth century.
6. Highly polished ivory seal-head-shaped nozzle for a sealskin float.
7. A sixteenth-century hourglass of the type used on board ship.
8. Ivory hafted flint harpoon head.
9. A diagrammatic representation of the 741-ton *Triumph*.
10. The Lower Pool looking across to Southwark.
11. A sixteenth-century long house of the type built by Wynter on Kodlunarn Island.
12. *The Alchemist* by Cornelis Pietersz Begijn, painted in 1663.
13. The generic memorial to Arctic explorers in King Edward VII Memorial Park, Shadwell.
14. A piece of ore taken from Meta Incognita.
15. A variant of the pistol carried by Frobisher in the painting by Cornelius Ketel.

List of Maps

Timeline of Frobisher and New World Exploration

1492   Columbus (Cristoforo Colon) lands on Guanahani Island in the Bahamas, renamed San Salvador
Columbus discovers that there is variation of the earth's magnetism when his compass deviates from True North

1493   Spanish Settlement of Hispaniola
Treaty of Tordesillas divides New World between Portugal and Spain
Columbus goes on to explore Puerto Rico, Cuba and Jamaica

1497   John Cabot on board the *Matthew* reaches Newfoundland

1498   Columbus discovers South American coast
Columbus sights the island of Trinidad and returns to Hispaniola to find the colony there wrecked by rebellion

1502   Portuguese navigators reach Brazil

1507   German cartographer Martin Waldseemüller publishes his *Cosmographia Introductio*, naming the New World America after Amerigo Vespucci

c. 1510   First African slaves brought to the Americas

1513   Spanish expedition under Vasco Balboa reaches Panama and sights the Pacific Ocean

1516   Italian scholar Peter Martyr's *Decades of the New World* discusses the importance of the discoveries in America

1519   Hernando Cortes begins conquest of Aztec Empire, introducing horses and firearms to the New World
Fernando Magellan sails from Spain with the task of finding a strait to the Pacific Ocean

1520	Fernando Magellan crosses the Pacific and reaches the island of Tierra del Fuego
1524	Florentine navigator Giovanni de Verrazzano explores the coast of North America including New York, Nova Scotia and Newfoundland for Francis I of France
	Sebastian de Belalcazar conquers Nicaragua and Costa Rica
1526–9	English navigator Sebastian Cabot establishes a colony in Paraguay. The settlement is destroyed by natives
1527–8	Giovanni de Verrazzano is sent to collect brazilwood for dyes and is eaten by Carib cannibals on the Island of Guadeloupe
1528–46	German colony established at Caracas, Spanish South America, led by Ambrosius Alfinger
1530	Spanish conquistador Francisco de Montejo begins the conquest of the Pacific coast of Mexico
1531	Francisco Pizarro begins conquest of Inca Empire
1533	Fifteen hereditary captaincies set up in Brazil by John III of Portugal
1534	French navigator Jacques Cartier lands on Anticosti Island in the Gulf of St Lawrence, claiming the territory as New France
1535	Pizarro founds a colony near Lima on the Pacific coast of South America
1535–6	Cartier's second expedition to the St Lawrence River reaches Montreal but is turned back by the appalling winter and attacks from natives
	Probable birth date of Martin Frobisher
1540	A Spanish expedition under Francisco de Coronado searches present-day Arizona, New Mexico and Texas for mythical cities
1541	A Spanish expedition under Hernando de Soto finds the Mississippi River
	Spanish soldier of fortune Pedro de Valdivia founds

	Santiago de Chile, capital of modern Chile
1543	Spanish navigator Luis de Moscoso discovers oil in what is now Texas
	A second attempt by the French to found a settlement along the St Lawrence River is abandoned because of the harsh winter
	Wheat, barley and cattle introduced to South America
1544	Blasco de Vela publishes a new law in Lima to improve living conditions for the natives
1545	Discovery of silver mines at Potosi (Peru) and Zacatecas (Mexico)
1549	Mercury is discovered in Peru
	Martin Frobisher moves to London
1553	**Martin Frobisher accompanies Thomas Wyndham to Guinea (First Guinea Expedition)**
1554	**Martin Frobisher accompanies Second Guinea Expedition**
1558	Italian author Giovanni Ramusio publishes *On Navigations and Voyages*, the first widely read account of voyages in the New World
1559	**Martin Frobisher marries Isobel Rigett**
	Martin Frobisher possibly working as a government spy
	Martin Frobisher imprisoned for piracy in Launceston Gaol
c. 1560	Portuguese begin sugar cultivation in Brazil
1561	The Muscovy Trading Company publishes Cortes' *The Art of Navigation* for the first time
1562	A French colony under Jean Ribault is settled at Charlesfort in modern-day Florida
1562–3	**Martin Frobisher accompanies John Hawkins on the first English slave-trading expedition to the Caribbean via Guinea, Africa**
1563	Jean Ribault presents his *True Discoverie of Terra Florida* to the English court

1564	**Second slave-trading voyage of Hawkins and Frobisher sails from Plymouth**
c. **1565**	Introduction of the potato to England
1565	**Martin Frobisher carries out privateering raids on Spanish ships**
1566	John Hawkins introduces tobacco to the English court
1568	Flemish cartographer Gerardus Mercator devises the cylindrical map projection for use on sea charts
1569	**Martin Frobisher imprisoned for piracy in the Fleet and the Marshalsea**
1570	Flemish cartographer Abraham Ortelius publishes the first modern atlas
1571	Spaniards conquer the Philippines **Martin Frobisher commands a privateering fleet in the Channel** **Martin Frobisher works for the government as part of the attempt to pacify Ireland**
1572	A collection of writings on alchemy, *Of the gold yielding act which is called chemistry*, is published in Basle
1573	**Martin Frobisher involved in spurious espionage plots to capture Flushing and kidnap the Catholic rebel Thomas Stanley**
1576	English scientist Robert Norman discovers the magnetic 'dip' in a compass needle **Martin Frobisher leads the first voyage in search of a North-West Passage to China** **Martin Frobisher brings the first Inuit to England**
1577	English expedition under Francis Drake rounds the world via Cape Horn and attacks Spanish settlements and shipping on the way to search for the North-West Passage **Martin Frobisher leads the second voyage to Meta Incognita**

1596	Tomatoes are introduced into England from America, purely as decoration because they are believed to be poisonous
	Wheeled vehicles introduced to America by Spanish colonists
1599	English mathematician Edward Wright calculates actual distances from Mercator's distorted projection
1602	Merchant captain George Weymouth maps the New England coast
1604	French explorer Samuel de Champlain founds a colony in Passamaquoddy Bay (modern-day Maine)
1606	English expedition under Christopher Newport and John Smith reach Chesapeake Bay
1607	First permanent English settlement in America at Jamestown, Virginia established by Christopher Newport
1607–8	The Plymouth Company attempts to establish an English colony on the Maine coast
1608	French colonists under Samuel de Champlain found Quebec
	English explorer John Smith publishes *A True relation of Virginia*
	The first glass beads are made at Jamestown for trade with the natives
1609	The telescope is invented in Holland
	English explorer Henry Hudson fails to find a North-West Passage for the Dutch East India Company
1611	Henry Hudson dies near Hudson Bay
1612	Charter granted to the Virginia Company of London to hold a lottery to raise funds for colonising Virginia
	John Smith produces detailed maps of the coast of North America
	Virginia planter John Rolfe is the first Englishman to grow tobacco in Virginia

1613   Dutch merchants establish a permanent trading post
            on Manhattan Island
1614   Dutch merchants form the New Netherland
            Company of Amsterdam trade along the Hudson
1615   Rubber is imported from South America
1617   Second expedition to the Orinoco in search of gold
1618   Dutch trappers settle on site of present-day Jersey
            City
            Virginia exports 20,000lb of tobacco
            First serious outbreak of smallpox in the New World
            decimates native American communities
1619   First Africans in North America arrive as indentured
            servants in Virginia
1620   The *Mayflower* lands in New England

Prologue

Shadwell, May 1578

John Thorne told the Captain-General he was fourteen. In fact, he didn't know how old he was, but the older he appeared, the more likely it was that the Captain-General would take him on. All day he had waited on the Shadwell quayside, with wadding in his pattens to make him look taller. He had coughed a little when the men gave him a pipe, but the beer tasted good enough and he enjoyed their tall tales. Mountains of ice indeed! Lights that glowed in the sky! For as long as he could remember, he'd been hearing stories like that. Men with no heads and with faces in their chests; mermaids that sang their sadness from far rocks; spouting leviathans that swallowed ships whole. Most of it, he'd noticed, came from men in their cups and the more they drank the taller the tales became.

The Master seemed a fair man. He smiled a lot and clapped him on the back, calling him 'Master Thorne'. But the Captain-General was something else. He had a beard like mouldy straw and when he walked the planks of his quarter-deck, the earth shook. John had never heard an accent like his in all his twelve summers. He spoke slowly, with long vowels, looking each of the hands up and down. Then, he got to John. He looked at his pattens, looked at the skinny legs in the darned hose, the doublet and pantaloons that were hand-me-downs from his brother. He looked for a long time into the boy's face and smiled at his fur hat. Then he saw the drum.

'Beat to quarters,' he growled.

John swung the drum to his side, whipped the sticks from the leather and brought them thudding down to the taut skin. The sound rattled across the decks of the Ayde *to the quayside, where the derricks swung and the pigs squealed as they were driven aboard. No one jumped to attention. No one ran to the guns. Everybody knew this was a test, the Captain-General taking on his crew. The man's hand flew up from his sword-hilt to command silence and the boy stopped.*

'If you're fourteen,' he snarled, leaning forward, 'I'm the Pope's
arse. Have you a mother living?'

John clicked the sticks away and stood looking at him. 'Sir?'

The Captain-General leaned back. 'Never mind.' He looked at the
clerk beside him. 'Can you sign?' he asked the boy.

'No, sir,' John said.

'What's your name?'

'John Thorne, sir.'

The clerk's quill scratched it down.

'Make your mark,' the clerk said.

John took the quill and made the sign of the cross where he assumed
his name had been written. He had never seen it written down before.

The Captain-General leaned sideways. 'Well, John Thorne,' he
said, smiling now. 'Do you think you can drum like that with a
hundred savages running at you, waving their spears and harpoons?'

John gulped. 'I think so, sir,' he said.

'And do you think you can drum like that when this ship sails like a
ghost in the thickest fog you ever saw? Where the ice stands a hundred
feet above the topmast? When the only other sound you'll hear is your
own heart?'

John gulped again but this time could not find the words.

The Captain-General folded his arms. 'If you've a mother living,
lad,' he said, 'Best say goodbye to her. Tell her you're going to Meta
Incognita. Can you remember that?'

'Yes sir,' said John.

The Captain-General waved him away, then stood up and called,
'And tell her Martin Frobisher will do his best to bring you back.'

The Ice Sea, July 1578

John Thorne shivered at his post on the main deck. The fur hat he had
brought with him seemed useless now. His ears were already nipped and
cut with frostbite and his lips were blue with cold. Never in all his life
had he felt cold like it and it had got worse day by day. Ever since
Friesland, the ice had thickened. He had survived the storms, the
lurching of the Ayde and the hail that stung like stones, pounding on
the canvas and bouncing off the planks awash with water.

But he had never seen anything like this. The Ayde, *the men had told him, displaced 240 tons and carried thirty cannon, sakers and demi-culverins. For the past two months, the ship had been his home. Now he could see how small it was, a little dark dot in the midst of this great silent sea. No one spoke on deck. The Captain-General and the Master, men who had seen all this before, stood in their cloaks on the quarter deck, staring at the whiteness before them.*

It looked like land, but it was not land. It was a series of huge white bergs, like floating castles. Any one of them could crush the Ayde *to matchsticks. Here and there were fragments of sludge, ice saturated by the sea, sliding past the wake of the* Ayde *and rolling in the waters. Ice the men called rotten was riddled with holes, as though the dons had blasted it with grapeshot. The bergs were emeralds and sapphires, great jewels that John had heard the queen of England owned.*

The sky was as white as the bergs, slashed here and there with a clear blue where the water channels ran. John Thorne did not know it but the old hands were looking for the yellow light, the land blink. That at least meant rock below your feet and a roaring fire to warm by.

And everyone knew they had all come for the gold. This land the Captain-General called Meta Incognita was a mountain of gold. Where was it, among all this wilderness, with its blindness of snow?

There was a roar far away that shattered the silence. It was a berg, cracking, crumbling, falling away from its sisters, sliding into the sea. The wash from the distant fall rocked the Ayde. *And then silence again. John looked up at the hard features of the Captain-General, frost settling on his beard and eyebrows, his eyes scanning the horizon. John's life, the life of every man on board depended on him, as it had from that first day on Shadwell Quay.*

Because he was the Captain-General. He was Martin Frobisher.

From unremarkable beginnings Frobisher came to advise Queen Elizabeth on matters of international trade and travelled to the largely unknown and treacherous continent of Africa. By the time he was nineteen, he was a prisoner of and by turns a negotiator for the Portuguese.

He does not share the celebrity or notoriety of Ralegh or Drake. Whether this is due to inconsistencies in the historical record relating to his life, or because he was both a success and failure, he does nevertheless play a role in the development of England's place as a world power. We know little of Frobisher the man. He gained little from his education, had a quick temper and was lauded for his physical strength. He was married twice, but not much else is known of his private life. We know more of Frobisher the explorer, the playmaker, the figurehead. This book is not a glorification of a maritime hero or unique explorer, because Frobisher is neither. True, he gained fame against the Armada, and was involved in the romanticized privateering (some would say piracy) of the day. He was also instrumental in raising interest in North America and Canada, helping to create a fascination for a new part of the world that was to become hugely significant. However, his actual motivations, successes and failures, such as his erroneous discovery of gold deposits (which turned out to be useless pyrite) and his imprisonment for theft of a cargo of wine, make him seem more human than his edified contemporaries.

The merchants of England were constantly looking to create new means of expanding commerce, with as much exclusivity as possible. For example, the wool trade in England was strong and English commodities reached as far as the African coast, but this was via Portuguese merchants selling them on from English traders in the Iberian markets. This is one of the reasons why, after a few years, Frobisher was able to gain support for his voyages to find the North-West Passage. Coupled with this was the emerging notion of territorial acquisitions. Most of the individuals engaged in exploration, Frobisher included, were largely in it for personal gain. However, as the sixteenth century reached its final decades, the focus shifted to creating new lands that could be colonized, spreading England's influence across the globe. Frobisher's voyages to Canada bridge this gap between increasing wealth and trade and territorial expansion.

This book charts a life that encapsulated the major issues of an era: the importance of an expanding world, and England's part in it; the history of exploration in hitherto largely uncharted territory, and the society, economics and politics of the age. It also stretches beyond the machinations of Europe. The lasting marks on the landscape where Frobisher set up mining works and colonies in Canada are still visible. They hold a place in the oral tradition of the indigenous peoples, the Inuit, with whom Frobisher had some of the first contact. The paintings of John White and the writings of George Best and Dionysus Settle, who travelled with Frobisher, create a surprisingly clear (if biased) picture of a newly discovered culture.

Boys like John Thorne, who sailed with Frobisher, are part of his legend. We know almost nothing about them because history rarely records the opinions and feelings and experiences of the common man. Yet Martin Frobisher was a common man too and to learn about Frobisher is to learn about his crews, his friends, his enemies and the world in which he lived.

Others followed Frobisher in search of a North-West Passage and did it better – or perhaps luck was with them – but his contribution is unique. In our jaded world, where the travels of a lifetime are commonplace and we fume about delayed flights and cramped aircraft and can see the polar landscape on film or television, we can never hope to share that sense of wonder that John Thorne felt on the deck of the *Ayde*, sailing through the silence of a dazzling and terrible new world with Martin Frobisher.

Chapter 1

North-country Boy

The Frobisher family are first heard of in Scotland in the early thirteenth century. The name may derive from the Norman French *fourbisseur*, swordsmith, and such surnames usually originated in a nickname ascribed to an individual based on his profession. About 1260, John Frobisher was rewarded with lands near Chirk in Denbighshire by Edward I for his part in the Welsh border campaigns. The King was anxious to subdue the Welsh before turning on the Scots and under the feudal system, knights like Frobisher were expected to supply arms, men and their own personal services. Edward's system was to build a series of castles along the Welsh border and around the coast to keep the Welsh in check. One of these was the castle at Chirk, erected by the Marcher Lord Roger Mortimer in 1295.

It might be expected then that John's descendant, Martin Frobisher, came from a fine military tradition, particularly when considering his exploits later in life. In fact, the Frobishers were not military heroes, nor hugely ambitious. In the mid-fifteenth century Thurston Frobisher, whose name is variously spelt Furbisher, Ffourbyssher, Furbiser and Frobisher, moved to West Yorkshire. At least forty-one contemporary spellings of this name can be found in the Elizabethan period. It was not the safest of times. Within a decade, the county became one of the focal points of open warfare in the baronial feuds known as the Wars of the Roses and, not for the last time, the Frobishers found themselves caught up in the net of national politics.

Little is known of the family until another John married Joan, the daughter of a powerful local dignitary, Sir William Scargill, who was steward of Pontefract Castle, usually known as Pomfret in the sixteenth century and traditionally the murder site of King Richard II. This marriage brought a dowry comprising the manor of Altofts, near Normanton, a few miles from Wakefield. The estate no longer exists in the contemporary landscape, and neither is it mentioned extensively in the written record, although its name, of Viking origin and meaning 'old house', suggests that the house and estate had been in existence for some time. The estate's significance to the legend of Martin Frobisher is arguable beyond serving as a place to begin his chronology, as he only spent his uneventful formative years there until his early teens. Frobisher was the third of five children – his siblings were John, David, Jane and Margaret – and we know that his father, Bernard, died prematurely in August 1542, when Martin was probably aged seven years. He left the care of his wife and children to his elder brother Francis, who was Recorder and Mayor of Doncaster by this time.

Martin's mother was Margaret, née Yorke, of Gowthwaite, descended from a family that had endeared itself to the Tudor royal family to the extent that Richard Yorke had been knighted by Henry VII in 1487, the year that marked the de facto end of the Wars of the Roses.

The humanist scholar John Leland travelled extensively throughout England between 1539 and 1545 and provides a fascinating snapshot of Martin Frobisher's county when he was a small boy. Leland in fact visited Yorkshire twice, many of its monastic houses having already disappeared in what was the high-water mark of Henry VIII's Dissolution of the Monasteries. He was not merely passing through, but criss-crossed the largest county in England, taking in the Wakefield area of the Frobishers in 1539.

Leland was struck by the town's nine-arched bridge over the Calder. On it, he recorded, as though very aware of the sudden passing of the medieval church, was a chapel dedicated to 'Our Lady' with a foundation for two chantry priests. Conscious of his history, the traveller mentioned the 'fearful battle' fought in the Wars of the Roses in the fields to the south of the bridge and recalled the cross erected on the road that wound up into the town that marked the death scene of Richard, Duke of York. Locals in the area still referred to the battle's victor, Lord Clifford, as 'the butcher'.

All Saints' Church was new in Leland's day, and described as 'exceptionally fine and large' with a separate vicarage. He visited Lowe Hill beyond the town, where legend had it that the Warre family tried to build, but the wind kept blowing their work over. The town centre, which the Frobishers must have known well, was largely timber built, but some areas were of stone. 'There are few inland towns in Yorkshire,' Leland wrote, 'that can boast a better site or surroundings.'[1]

In common with the rest of the county, the 'coarse cloth industry' was the mainstay of the economy, but, in an unconscious nod to the future, Leland also observed the coal pits on Wakefield Moor. Infuriatingly, Leland mentions the parish of Altofts, but not the Frobishers, concentrating instead on the Mallett family, clearly neighbours of the Frobishers, who owned land there.

Martin Frobisher, who seems never to have become fully literate, always gave his date of birth as 1539. However, since the Secretary of State, Thomas Cromwell, introduced the first parish registers in that year and Frobisher's name is not listed, then it is much more likely that he was born in about 1535 or 1536. The first significant male figure in Martin's life of whom we have evidence was his father's uncle, Francis. Like his brother, Francis married well, to Christiana Hastings, daughter of the Sheriff of Yorkshire. He rose to local prominence as the Mayor of Doncaster, and counted amongst his friends the Earl of Southampton and Lord Admiral of England, William Fitzwilliam. In an age of patronage, such ties were vital. Fitzwilliam also came from a relatively obscure Yorkshire family and his links with both the court of Henry VIII and the Navy were to have major, if indirect, influence on the career of Martin Frobisher. Since the Frobishers came from and lived in a relatively landlocked area, there has to be some reason to explain Frobisher's subsequent passion. Other 'seadogs' of the day, like Drake and Ralegh, had much more obvious seafaring connections.

We do not know whether Francis encouraged or even fully supported Martin and this is further highlighted when, on the death of his mother in 1549, Martin was sent from the family home to live in London with his uncle by marriage, Sir John Yorke. Whether this was a calculated move on the part of Francis is again questionable. Martin appears to have received little education, or at least not benefited greatly from it. Exactly what sort of schooling he had is unknown. For example, two of his neo-contemporaries, Christopher Marlowe and William Shakespeare, went to their local schools in Canterbury and Stratford respectively. This was thirty years later, however, and a different generation. Marlowe's quick wit and lovely singing voice made him a natural for the King's School and Corpus Christi, Cambridge, whereas Shakespeare, the son of a higher status family, attended his local grammar school, learned little Latin and less Greek and did not go on to university.

It is at least likely that young Martin was taught at home. He would certainly have been an accomplished horseman and able to handle himself with a sword. In a society where religion still mattered, it can be assumed that Martin would have had enough of a grasp of literacy to cope with the prayer book and other elements of compulsory church attendance. Was the move to London an attempt to educate him in the art of commerce under the tutelage of the powerful merchant Yorke? There is a tradition that schools in Yorkshire were inadequate, but it seems just as likely that Francis wanted rid of the burden of his brother's offspring. Whatever the case, it was in London that Frobisher was exposed to notions of commerce, trade, influence and power.

Martin Frobisher had never left his native county and at the age of 14, with no awareness of the capital, the journey alone must have been a daunting prospect. We do not know how he travelled. One way would have been to take a ship from the Humber, hugging the coast to the Thames, rather as sea coal was transported from the coal fields of Durham. If so, this must have been Martin's first exposure to any kind of sea travel and perhaps it thrilled him to the extent that he wanted to repeat the experience in a rather more daredevil way. Alternatively, he could have travelled by horseback along the Great North Road, staying at any of the already established coaching towns on the way. The first of these, crossing the River Witham (then known as Lindis), was Grantham. He would have ridden past the thirteenth-century parish church of St Wulfrum and perhaps stayed at the Angel Inn, which once belonged to the Templars. The market cross and Conduit House, which provided water for the town, were new in Frobisher's time. From there, he would have travelled to Huntingdon on the Ouse and would have been exactly 59 miles from King's Cross, still with three days of his journey to go. The bridge he would have ridden over had been built in 1332, but the town's castle had already fallen into disuse. He may have stayed at an inn called the George, which by the eighteenth century was a full-blown galleried coaching inn. The road took him south through Biggleswade to Ware on the Lea. Perhaps he stayed at the Saracen's Head, famous for its associations with the town's Great Bed. One more day would see him in London.

At the end of the decade in which Martin came to London, Ralph Agas drew a comprehensive panorama of the city. The medieval wall was still largely intact, demarcating what was essentially the Roman square mile. To the east, north of the Tower, green fields flourished around Aldgate and the areas to the north were still known by their parish names and the nearest gate. Bishopsgate led north-east to Cambridge, Cripplegate lay to the east of the great church of

St Bartholomew and the old tournament ground of Smithfield. Along the river, the palaces of the great and good jostled with the warehouses and wharfs that contributed indirectly to their wealth.

A north-country lad like Frobisher would have been astonished by the size, noise and bustle of the city. The Dissolution of the Monasteries in the 1530s had created open spaces where the 'cities of God' had once stood, their stone bought up cheaply for secular buildings. The resulting waste ground was encroached upon by vagrants – the 'many-headed monster' composed of the sturdy beggars that the Tudor government so feared. Ditches were being filled in and undulating ground levelled. Streams like the Fleet and the Wall Brook were open cesspits but would have disappeared by the end of the century.

The churches dominated the skyline; St Paul's was the biggest in the world and still retained the spire that would fall to a lightning strike in 1561. Henry VIII's new palace of the Bridewell dominated the north bank to the west of Baynard's Castle, a reminder of the sprawling power of the monarchy and the fact that the principal buildings of London were best reached by the army of watermen who ferried the river.

John Stow, who was ten years older than Martin Frobisher, was born on a farm in Aldgate and left a fascinating record of the city in his day. The City proper was the heart of a rapidly growing commerce and was essentially where Frobisher's future lay. To the west, a new 'West End' was developing with inhabitants of the professional classes, more homogenous than the City where 'Dives lay down with Lazarus'. Across the river in Southwark were the shipwrights and sailors who would supply Frobisher with his crews. Here, too, were the theatres that delighted Shakespeare's audiences and the brothels that provided entertainment for those out on the tiles.

Though he did not arrive in London as a Dick Whittington character coming to 'seek his fortune', it was a much more suitable sphere for the young lad, quick of temper and with a

clear love of adventure. Further to this, he was surrounded by
the influential powerful merchant organizations through one
of its leading lights. Sir John Yorke was part of that dynamic
world, the upwardly mobile merchant class that is associated
with the Tudors. Henry VIII's policy of choosing new men
from relatively humble backgrounds had its knock-on effect
throughout society and in Martin Frobisher's early years there
was an unprecedented rise in individual enterprise. Along the
Thames, Queenshithe and Billingsgate were the major quays,
but ocean-going ships increasingly set sail from Henry VIII's
new dock at Deptford, from Wapping and Ratcliffe. Merchants
moved into the derelict monastic buildings, evicting the ragged
squatters. The Leathersellers' Company grabbed St Helen's
Bishopsgate and the Butchers' Guild bought up St Nicholas in
1549. By the end of the century, there were forty-seven
guildhalls in London, each of them vying with the other in
terms of opulence.

John Yorke was a formidable character, a shrewd and
ruthless financier, who amassed not only a vast fortune, but
significant political influence. His home was in the Walbrook,
on the site of the ancient stream that ran into the Thames.
During his time in the markets of Europe, Yorke, like many
English merchants, had an ear open for talk that might damage
or benefit England, from invasion plots to finding lucrative
new markets. It was information of this type that saw Thomas
Cromwell appoint him Master Assayer at the Tower Mint.
Since the thirteenth century the Royal Mint was based in
London, replacing provincial mints dotted around the country.
So prestigious was this institution that it provided not only
coins for Britain, but, in the reign of Mary Tudor, for her
husband Philip II's Spain too. From this position, Yorke was
able to control the flow of silver into the City, giving him huge
influence. He managed to remain at the Mint, even after his
patron Cromwell fell from grace.

'Master' Cromwell had arguably risen too far and too fast.
The son of a blacksmith and brewer from Putney, he was

doubling as a scrivener and lawyer from 1513 and joined the household of Cardinal Wolsey the following year. An MP by 1523, he was a prime mover in the Dissolution of the Monasteries and rose rapidly in the service of the King. He was a privy councillor by 1531, Chancellor of the Exchequer two years later and Master of the Rolls the year after that. His power was huge and he did not care who he trod on to maintain it. 'The hammer of the monasteries' in effect helped his King to create a Protestant church (although this was probably never Henry's intention). Cromwell saw the supremacy of the secular power over it. But his handling of the King's marriage to the notoriously unsuitable Anne of Cleves proved his undoing. Henry loathed the 'Flanders mare' on sight and Cromwell, now Earl of Essex, was stripped of his titles and executed in 1540.

In an age of patronage, men like Yorke rode on greater men's coat tails and either by luck or because he was good at his job, he held on. From this position of power, as well as through his success as a merchant, Yorke's influence continued to expand. He loaned many powerful dignitaries money, including Edward Seymour, Lord Somerset, the Lord Protector of England. Henry VIII's death in January 1547 left a boy king on the throne and the void was filled by Somerset as effective regent. Since Edward VI was young it seemed natural and sensible for his uncle to take on this role. Somerset was a warrior, intent on keeping the marauding Scots in their place, and a Protestant, furthering that cause throughout the country. Whether it was an argument over the loan or a testament to his radical and changeable politics, Yorke became a staunch and instrumental supporter of Somerset's rival and successor, the Earl of Warwick.

Warwick was John Dudley, ex-captain of Calais, the only part of France still controlled by England, and a former comrade of Somerset's. What happened in 1549 was a straight power-play between these two co-regents with the same ambition. The Earl's campaign and plans against Somerset were conducted from Yorke's house. Yorke used his financial clout to raise money in support of Warwick, and was also able to levy aid by repaying loans made by Antwerp merchants to England. Although this endeared him to the merchant population of the city, and obviously supporters of Warwick, he put himself in a dangerous position as Protector Somerset was a public favourite. However, his risky gamble paid off when Somerset was imprisoned and executed in 1552, and he became Sir John Yorke, knighted by Edward VI himself in the merchant's own home. He even survived a spell in the Tower, near his own Mint, after Warwick's ill-fated attempt to place his daughter-in-law, Jane Grey, on the throne, in place of Henry VIII's daughter, Mary. Yorke clearly had a knack for survival. In the maelstrom of Tudor politics, life was cheap and loyalties shifted easily. Jane Grey, the 'nine days' queen', is remembered as a political pawn and martyr, but she was probably just as astute and ambitious as the men of her family. As the 16-year-old Edward lay dying, probably of tuberculosis, Jane was married against her will to Lord Guildford Dudley, Warwick's fourth son, as part of a scheme to ensure a Protestant succession. The unmarried, childless Edward would be replaced by the rabid Catholic Mary, his elder sister and that promised a bloodbath for Protestants. Yorke was imprisoned more for his affiliation with Warwick, rather than for being involved in the plot. This meant that he would not stay behind bars for long and his ability to garner influence saw him in the position of Sheriff of London by the time of Martin's arrival.

Far from being a nurturing father figure, it is clear that Yorke's influence rubbed off on his young charge. Although Frobisher had a rudimentary education, the fiscal and financial skills he developed proved useful when convincing investors to support his explorations. Hot-headed and impulsive, it was as part of Yorke's expeditions that Martin was able to indulge his adventurous spirit, and also become an experienced explorer and able seaman. Because of the position that his uncle held, he was able to gather round him an influential clique of supporters, such as the Loks. The Loks hailed from Cheapside and were an entrepreneurial family at the cutting edge of the merchant-venture movement of their day. They had a flourishing business in Flanders, and did not return to England during the reign of Mary Tudor because they were recent converts to Protestantism and therefore would have been natural targets of the Queen. During these years, it is unclear how Yorke used the young Frobisher's talents.

As a cloth merchant, Yorke was involved in the lucrative European markets. England was the primary wool-producing nation in the world, and it was a focus of commerce with Antwerp and Calais. Although this trade in wool made fortunes for English merchants, it became increasingly apparent that the English were losing out on expanding markets. For instance, the Spanish and Portuguese were selling on the cloth to Africa, the East and the New World. This, including taxes and restrictions imposed by the controlling bodies of the European markets, meant that England's trade was suffering. The situation was exacerbated when, in the 1550s with wool production at its height, the bottom fell out of the market and supply far outstripped demand. This forced London's merchants to seek other means of increasing trade. Some had already considered other avenues, by becoming involved in expeditions from Spain and Portugal to Hispaniola and the Canaries. A generation earlier, with the old silk and spice roads to the East cut off by the Ottoman Turks, European explorers had turned West to find an alternative sea route. That had led to the discovery and exploration of the West Indies and the Americas. Portuguese explorers da Gama and de Covilha concentrated on the West African coast in the last years of the fifteenth century, looking for gold, slaves and spices, whilst Vespucci and Ojeda sailed West to find the Spice Islands. Although nominally accepting Spanish and Portuguese rule, many English merchants returned home with their wares. This did not go unnoticed by the Spaniards, and as their non-European markets expanded, their control of who was trading, and where they conducted that trade, tightened.

In 1530, William Hawkins, a successful merchant sailor from Plymouth, mounted an expedition to Brazil and the coast of Guinea. The area had been discovered thirty years earlier by Pedro Cabral and the line of demarcation decided upon arbitrarily by Pope Alexander VI gave Brazil to Portugal. One of Hawkins' initial undertakings was to obtain dyewood from Brazil (the area's main export initially), to be used in the still lucrative cloth trade in England. His voyages, which cost an initial £23 to set up, returned with over £600 of commodities including 'elephant's teeth' from the Ivory Coast. His son John Hawkins continued this lucrative legacy as well as plundering Spanish and Portuguese ships during the 1560s. In 1552, a Portuguese vessel found its way into English waters. Its cargo of gold and spices further sparked merchants' interest in these new markets. So it was in 1553 that Sir John Yorke and a number of fellow merchants began preparations to mount an expedition to the west coast of Africa. They chose Thomas Wyndham to lead it.

Wyndham was an obvious choice because, in 1551, he, like Hawkins before him, had experienced the South American and West African markets. In particular, he had visited Barbary, or Morocco, which was renowned for sugar and saltpetre, used in the production of gunpowder. In these treacherous waters the weather was not the only enemy. The Portuguese believed that the area belonged to them exclusively and they in turn were challenged by the fearsome Barbary pirates on whom none could count as allies. They were variously Moorish, French and English and they preyed on European trading vessels. Wyndham had a number of Portuguese pilots in his employ. The Portuguese were considered the ablest and most-experienced sailors of the age. In a time when in England little was known of climate or methods of navigation, Portuguese mercenary sailors were valued for their skills. Perhaps the most famous of these was John Cabot, who had been unable to find funding in his adopted homeland of Spain. However, under English auspices he became the first to explore the coast of North America in the late 1490s.

The high-profile nature of this expedition, which was formed of three ships – the *Lion of London*, the *Primrose* and the *Moone* – with a crew of over 140, reached the ears of the Portuguese ambassadors in London. Keen to protect their monopoly, they attempted to stop the expedition. The political climate could not have been more perfect from their point of view. Edward VI had died that year, and Yorke, previously a major investor in the expedition, had been imprisoned, implicated in Warwick's treason. Further to this, the new Queen, Mary, was married to Philip of Spain. Perhaps, if this expedition had been attempted a couple of years later, the Portuguese would have been successful in stopping it, as an Anglo-Spanish court would have been keen to placate their neighbour. As it was, it is possible that this time of upheaval was too perfect. Whilst all the changes and political strife were playing out, the remaining financiers of the expedition quietly went ahead with their preparations, and in August 1553, the voyage was underway, with Wyndham in command. The crew included several merchants, there to protect their investment and investigate potential new markets.

Amongst them, the 18-year-old Martin Frobisher.

Chapter 2

From Prisoner to Pirate

For Frobisher, the first and second voyages to Guinea instilled the 'merchant adventurer' in him. Although not a gifted financier like his uncle, Frobisher was nevertheless likely to have been very much involved in the day-to-day running of the ship, especially as he was almost the youngest crew member. What Frobisher lacked in education, he made up for with shrewdness and cunning. His exact role was assistant to his uncle's factor (steward) John Beryn.

Thanks to the extraordinary salvage job and underwater archaeology associated with the *Mary Rose*, sunk in 1545 and raised from the Solent in 1982, a great deal is now known about seafaring in Tudor times. William Harrison was no doubt more than a little biased when he wrote in the year before the Armada: 'And therefore the common report that strangers make of our ships amongst themselves is daily confirmed to be true, which is that for strength, assurance, nimbleness and swiftness of sailing, there are no vessels in the world to be compared with ours.'[1] In reality, life aboard a Tudor ship was nasty, brutish and short. It was only possible to walk upright on the upper decks and there were no hammocks until the mid-1590s. Food was salted pork or beef, with biscuits that acquired the consistency of porridge when riddled with weevils. The all-important water, carried in guarded barrels, turned sour after a while and contributed to myriad diseases to which sailors fell prey.

At this point in his life, it is likely that Frobisher saw himself as a merchant first and foremost. Years later, Nicholas Breton wrote of such a man:

> Upon a wooden horse he rides through the world and in
> a merry gale he makes a path through the seas. He is the
> discoverer of countries and a finder out of commodities,
> resolute in his attempts and royal in his expenses. He is
> the life of traffic and the maintainer of trade, the sailor's
> master and the soldier's friend. He is the exercise of the
> exchange, the honour of credit . . . He fears not Scylla
> and sails close by Charybdis and having beaten out a
> storm, rides at rest in a harbour.[2]

Climbing rigging and hoisting sails would have appealed to
Frobisher's strong, feisty character. His physical strength is a
point of note from Dionysus Settle's account of the North-
West Passage voyages, and he was also commended for his
actions against the Armada (not to mention squaring up to
Francis Drake 'in his shirt' when that campaign was over).

One of the first undertakings was to secure supplies. To
make as much profit as possible, goods were not purchased for
the voyage, but instead obtained through raids on Portuguese
ports. This is something that would impact on the second
voyage, as it was one thing to conduct trade where the
Portuguese had a monopoly, but quite another to steal from
them. The waters around West Africa were already heavily
policed, and fortifications had been in place for nearly a
century. The port of Elmina, for instance, known to the
Portuguese as Sao Jorge de Mina (St George of the Mine) but
more commonly known as Fort Mina, was an imposing set-up
commanding control not only of the port, but also the
surrounding countryside. It had declared itself an independent
state and fiercely guarded the seaward and landward sides of its
territory. For an area that produced almost one-third of the
world's gold at the time, it is not surprising that such
fortifications existed. By openly attacking the Portuguese, the
English expedition was not doing itself, or those that followed,
any favours.

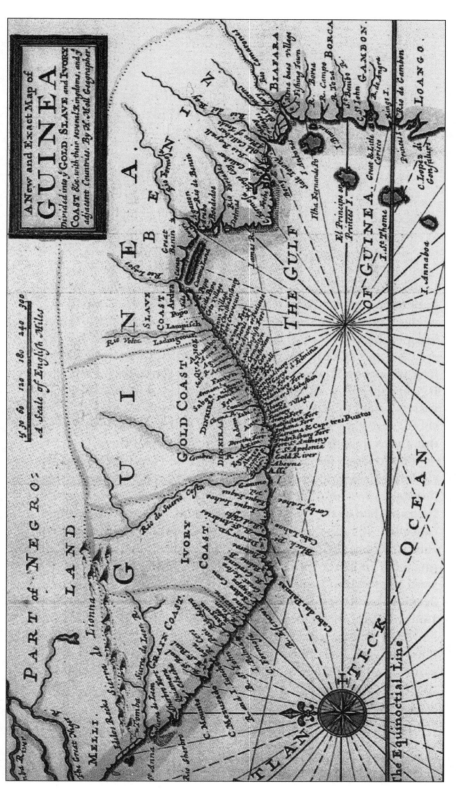

A near contemporary map of the Guinea Coast, vital to Europeans for its produce of gold, slaves and ivory.

However, angering the European colonists was the least of problems for the ill-fated expedition. Trade was conducted successfully in Barbary and Guinea, with cloth and timber being exchanged for gold, pepper, sugar and saltpetre. But greed had got the better of the captain, Thomas Wyndham. Progress was slow, and the voyage had fallen behind schedule. Against the advice of his more experienced Portuguese navigators, particularly Antonio Pinteado who openly opposed Wyndham's decision, they pushed further south in the face of the greatest danger, summer in West Africa. Throughout history climate has been one of explorers' worst enemies. Beyond storms at sea, extremes of hot and cold and a lack of understanding of tropical diseases decimated, even wiped out whole expeditions. Having reached Benin, one of the many independent states on the coast, and whilst trading pepper, the crew began to fall ill. The stubborn Wyndham was amongst the first to succumb, along with the wise but powerless Pinteado. By the time they came to leave, a number of pinnaces, small vessels used to carry crews and commodities from ship to shore, and the *Lion of London* herself had to be abandoned as there were insufficient sailors alive or fit to man them.

The journey home saw no respite from the climate, and on reaching England, fewer than forty men survived. Despite this disastrous loss of life, the expedition had been a commercial success, that in the eyes of the merchant investors more than cancelled out the death toll. This is an important thread that runs through Frobisher's story. Even the slightest hint of financial, and later territorial, gain meant than men and money were poured into these projects. Investors could still be found, despite the financial failure of previous expeditions. In the 1490s, John Cabot received funding for further expeditions to North America, although his first voyage ended in failure. Humphrey Gilbert, who was instrumental in championing and gaining support for Frobisher's voyages in 1578, had himself spectacularly failed in the attempt, driven back by storms earlier the same year.

The first expedition to Guinea was deemed a total success, but the lives of seamen were cheap. Thomas Nashe wrote of them in 1599:

> Voyages of purchase . . . which are now grown a common traffic, swallow up and consume more sailors and mariners than they breed and likely not a slop of a rope-hauler they send forth to the Queen's ships but he is first broken to the sea in the herring-man's skiff . . . where, having learned to brook all waters and drink as he can out of a terry can and eat poor John out of sooty platters, when he may get it, without butter or mustard, there is no ho with him . . . Some of these for their haughty climbing come home with wooden legs and some with none, but leave body and all behind.'[3]

By 1554, Yorke and a new group of investors, who would later form the Muscovy Company, were ready once again to set sail for the west coast of Africa. It appears that lessons had been learned from the previous voyage. The second expedition left in November 1554, an altogether more suitable time of year. This one was commanded by John Lok, even though his family was still living abroad for their own safety. This expedition was not to raid Portuguese ports, through fear of conflict, nor was it to press as far south as Benin, through fear of climate. Instead, it was to head straight for Guinea and the Gold Coast. Upon arrival, the English were faced with an indigenous population that had grown wise to the worth of what they had.

The area had been discovered in about 1440 and in conjunction with just about every other part of Africa, it became contested by European powers. Neighbouring Senegal had been discovered by the Portuguese in 1460. The tribal culture there was rich and diverse. Exquisite terracotta and bronze artwork has survived from this period, stylish designs that may have been copied from Portuguese books and intended for the oba (king). Between 1440 and 1473, the local ruler was Ewuare the Great, with his capital at Benin. Portuguese envoys were dealing with his successors from 1486 and if the image of ignorant savages being exploited by European greed was ever a reality, it was not true of the Gold Coast. The locals were wary of the anger of the Portuguese colonists, who were well established and wielded considerable military might along the coast. So it was that the tribesmen demanded a hostage of the English before negotiations could begin. Martin Frobisher volunteered.

At this stage, Frobisher can have had no real idea what captivity by the local tribesmen meant and it either speaks volumes for his heroism or his foolhardiness that he made the offer at all.

No such honourable negotiation was undertaken with the Portuguese, however, whose ships arrived in the port of Shamma at this crucial moment. They instantly attacked the English when coming upon their anchorage. The English successfully evaded the strike and fled back up the coast to England with a cargo of ivory, spices and 400lb of gold, with a comparatively small loss of twenty-four men, including the hapless hostage who now fell into the hands of the Portuguese.

Frobisher spent the next nine months in the cells at Fort Mina, but he was far from shackled. He gained significant knowledge of the area acting as a go-between to procure supplies from the local population, the Portuguese being far more willing to sacrifice an Englishman than one of their own. However, Frobisher was adept at this undertaking, showing his talent for interacting with indigenous tribes.

There is a sizeable gap in Frobisher's history during this period; nearly six years pass when not much is known of him. At some point he was moved from Mina to Lisbon, as a political prisoner was of little use in West Africa. The Portuguese capital was at that time one of the richest cities in the world, reflecting the huge maritime expansion of the nation. The old city that Frobisher would have known was a tortuous maze of streets, courts and alleyways, although a serious earthquake some twenty years earlier had led to recent rebuilding. It is by no means certain which prison housed the English hostage, but the conditions were appalling even by grim English standards.

In 1578 Richard Willes wrote that Frobisher's interest in the North-West Passage was sparked by conversations with his Portuguese inmates there, although this is not proven. It is just as likely to have been triggered by his increasing knowledge of exploration and his drive to further himself, for, penniless and, on his return to England, effectively homeless, he had amassed great experience as an explorer and negotiator. The method of his deliverance back home is uncertain. It is probable that he was aided by Anglo-Iberian merchants, perhaps aware of his background. Additionally, the young Frobisher, now in his early twenties, would have been of great use to merchants wishing to start their own voyages. The only real documentary evidence of Frobisher's movements in this period leading up to 1560 is from a naval report published in 1604. He is credited with delivering a hostage, Anthony Howard, from captivity in Barbary in 1559. This suggests that his services were indeed being employed back on the West African coast, whether as a mercenary or as a merchant is unclear.

In that year, on 30 September, Frobisher married Isobel, the widow of Thomas Rigatt, of Snaithe in his native Yorkshire. Isobel already had several children and no doubt an estate, which gave the 23-year-old Frobisher a sense of stability in an uncertain world. Perhaps because of their probable age difference or her brood of children, or possibly because of his adventurous spirit, the marriage was not happy. By the mid-1570s, Frobisher had abandoned both her and her children and he seems to have been totally unmoved by her death in a poor house in 1588. In an age of media scrutiny of the smallest flaw in those who aspire to celebrity, it seems almost unbelievable that a hero of the most dangerous and flamboyant military victory in a generation could leave his wife to die in penury without being brought to book. However, on this count Frobisher does not seem to have suffered at all at the hands of his peers or the public.

At about the time of his marriage he is known to have been present at court, where he provided information to Queen Elizabeth. Elizabeth was about three years older than Frobisher and although unused to the bluff accents and manners of the north, could hold her own with any man. If the pair met in 1560, the Queen had just recovered from a stormy start to her reign. Catholics hated her because her 'via media' Church of England was not likely to be a true compromise but a back-door method of creating a Protestant state. Others may have been hoping for a period of calm after the religious upheavals of the past decade, but public burnings still continued at Smithfield.

At a time when monarchs were expected to govern, Elizabeth needed to be kept informed of developments in other countries, especially when those countries were deadly rivals. Spanish and Portuguese trade in West Africa led her to condemn such a potential stranglehold being exercised by the two nations, and to refuse to stop English trade there, despite repeated protests from the ambassadors of those countries. This trading cold war was also certain to have contributed to the increase in privateering that occurred during this period.

Privateering was essentially a legalized form of piracy. Licences to act in this way were granted by the Crown and trade organizations who felt their interests were under threat. It gave ships carte blanche to seize cargoes and vessels of nations who posed a military or political challenge. In the 1560s, however, it was neither the Spanish nor the Portuguese against whom these licences were issued, but the French. During the reign of Mary, France and England had been in an on-off war with one another, continuing centuries of hostility and outright warfare. The last English stronghold in France,

Calais, was lost by Mary in 1558. This situation continued into Elizabeth's reign. English privateers, driven by the lure of wealth and possibly resentment of their other continental neighbours, also chose to attack Spanish, Portuguese and Dutch ships. In an attempt to stop these attacks, Margaret of Parma, Governor of the Netherlands from 1559, imposed embargos on English trade in her dominions. However, such embargos on a nation as powerful as England could not be sustained and made little difference to the situation. These strikes were initially openly condemned by Elizabeth, but the politics of the day were so fluid and full of mistrust that it seems highly likely that the privateers were in fact acting under her orders. Philip of Spain, for example, secretly supported both French and English. Over the next thirty years, the alliances and relationships between Europe's major powers – Spain, Portugal, France, the Netherlands and England – were in a constant state of flux with religious, political and territorial wars shifting the balance of power.

When Martin Luther nailed his ninety-five theses condemning the rapacity of the Catholic Church to the door of Wittenberg cathedral in 1517, he ushered in over a century of warfare. Bewildered by the monster he had created, Luther retreated and let others, more extreme, more violent, establish Protestantism in the valleys and mountains of Europe. The Catholic Church fought back, via the *Index Prohibitorum*, which banned heretical books, the proselytizing zealotry of the Jesuits and the vicious vengeance of the Holy Inquisition.

Spain and the Italian states stayed firm, to the extent that the Inquisition came to be known as Spanish. France remained squarely behind the Pope, too, except for the Huguenot settlements around La Rochelle. The many states of 'Germany' resembled a patchwork on the religious map of the mid-century, Catholic priests alongside Lutheran pastors eyeing each other with undisguised hatred. The Netherlands became essentially Protestant, as did England. Ireland, always a difficult and dangerous backwater, stayed loyal to the Papacy. The Scottish clans were split down the middle.

Religious motivation can be discerned in virtually every conflict in Europe in the sixteenth and seventeenth centuries. The French Wars of Religion speak for themselves, but the revolt of the Netherlands can be seen in terms of Protestant Dutchman against Catholic Spaniard. The Thirty Years War that engulfed the German states and even the English Civil War of the 1640s had religious undertones.

But it was not simply the Reformation that led to chaos and upheaval. The sixteenth century was Spain's *sieclo d'oro*, a time in which Philip II's empire was still vaguely Holy and Roman. The ex-consort of Mary Tudor owned Spain, huge chunks of 'Germany', the Netherlands and untold territory in the Americas. Lesser nations were jealous of this power and of the silver ships that sailed the Atlantic and some of them took up the flag of republicanism and nationalism to break away from the empire. The Dutch revolt had enormous ramifications for other countries too, leading directly to the two Spanish armadas launched against England.

Niccolò Machiavelli was denounced in 1513 when he wrote *The Prince* and is still regarded in certain quarters today as a cynic without scruple. In fact, the book is a blueprint for sixteenth-century government and largely a fair portrayal of the *realpolitik* of the time. So, because it suited everybody's book, former enemies sent their ambassadors to the negotiating table in April 1559 to sign the Treaty of Cateau-Cambresis, a three-way undertaking between England, France and Spain. Three months later, a lance-tip thudded into the brain of Henri II, King of France in a tournament accident, leaving the government of that country open to intrigue and rebellion. In March 1562 a congregation of 1,200 Huguenots was massacred by the Catholic army of François, Duke of Guise, sparking the wars of religion, which spluttered on intermittently until 1580. In England, there were plots against the Queen, mounted in the name of her rival, Mary, Queen of Scots, and with the tacit approval of the Pope. In October 1572, in one of many reprisal raids against Dutch rebels in the Netherlands, the Duke of Alva butchered men, women and children in the towns of Mechelin and Zurphen; but this paled into insignificance by comparison with the murder of at least 25,000 Huguenots in Paris three months earlier on St Bartholomew's Day.

Plots on her life notwithstanding, Elizabeth's main problem, like that of any other European ruler, was to maintain some sort of balance of power. Given that Spain had the edge, she needed to keep Philip sweet, whilst politely refusing to accept his lukewarm offer of marriage. In terms of privateering, she could always protest her innocence and hang offenders out to dry – Niccolò Machiavelli would have been proud of her.

From time to time, therefore, she punished individuals. In 1559, one character who truly deserved the title of pirate stood before an English court. Henry Strangeways had three times previously escaped imprisonment or worse for attacking Spanish ships, doubtless through the intervention of high-placed friends, or a series of mock trials staged to hide the fact that he was acting under orders. He stood accused of mounting an attempted attack on Fort Mina in West Africa. On this occasion, feeling his time had run out, he implicated two co-conspirators – John Lok and Martin Frobisher. Although ultimately he was released and lived to die a free man, Strangeways' accusations were perhaps not so ill-founded. Frobisher knew the fort and the area well. He may well have harboured hostility towards his erstwhile jailers. It is also on record that he was in the area at the time, returning with Anthony Howard.[4] This may well have excused his being arrested or even questioned over the accusations, returning a hero as he did.

In his absence, Martin's brother, John, had gone into business with John Appleyard. The two had purchased three ships and by the time of Martin's return they, along with an associate of Strangeways, Cornishman Peter Killigrew, were acting under licence in the English Channel. By 1563 they had captured five French ships. Whilst working with the more reliable Killigrew, the two took a ship, the *Katherine*. This was again a Spanish ship, although they both pretended they thought it was French. A brief spell in prison was merely a formality. In 1565 a Spanish Ambassador accused Frobisher of attacking and looting a Spanish ship, the *Flying Spirit*. But again, he was not brought to justice. He had amassed a great profit for the Crown through these attacks on Spanish ships and with increasingly tense relations between Spain and England, the Admiralty referring to him as 'well known to Philip of Spain and as well hated as . . . Hawkins himself'. John Hawkins was feared by the Spanish for his attacks on their vessels in Africa during the 1560s and perhaps this explains why Frobisher was once again let off with little more than a slapped wrist. In 1566 he was prevented from embarking on an illegal voyage to Guinea, perhaps to engage in unlawful trading or raids; he was released almost as soon as he had been arrested. However, a more prolonged spell in prison was not far off.

    John Appleyard and some other merchants of Rye, where the Frobishers and their associates had been working, turned on Martin and John, accusing them of theft. A cargo of wine had gone missing from a French ship and unfortunately it was the property of an English wine merchant. Frobisher, who by now had a reputation for attacking French vessels, was implicated and sued. He and his brother were imprisoned in Launceston Gaol for three months in 1559. It is worthy of note that Peter Killigrew's family were often held accountable for such fencing or smuggling of cargoes. Indeed, John Killigrew avoided a similar fate to that of the Frobishers when he was caught with stolen wine in 1577, escaping only by reimbursing the owners.

    It may be that by the mid-1560s, Frobisher had developed a taste for privateering. Claiming that he was leading another trading expedition to Guinea, he set sail in 1565 on board the *Mary Flower*. The Admiralty Court, which periodically leapt into outraged action in order to appear impartial to foreign observers, arrested him and John for a second time. Where he was imprisoned is not recorded, but by the end of October 1566, Frobisher was free again. Rather in the manner that Francis Drake was to adopt in the next decade, he accepted a commission from Cardinal Chatillon to attack Catholic vessels in the pay of the Guise family.

By this time, the French Wars of Religion had engulfed not only France but had threatened the stability of Europe for four years. A highly complex clash of politics and religion, the wars degenerated into a series of factional disputes between the house of Bourbon and the house of Guise. Because both received foreign aid in terms of men, money and ships, adventurers like Frobisher were drawn in.

Commanding the *Robert*, he trawled the waters of the English Channel looking for his targets. He seems to have been indiscriminate in the ships that he boarded and was once again a man marked by the Admiralty. He was arrested, either in July or August 1569, whilst putting into the port at Aldeburgh to refit and imprisoned first in the Fleet and then in the Marshalsea.

In Frobisher's day, the Fleet, situated on a site that had become an open sewer flowing into the Thames, specialized in holding prisoners who owed money to the Crown. Such men had usually been committed by the Queen's Council or Court of Chancery and had not offended under common law or statute. Frobisher's position was potentially very serious – engaging in military service for a foreign power without the express consent of the monarch could result in death.

Six years before Frobisher was sent there, the keepership of the prison had been sold for a staggering £8,000, a reminder that most London prisons were business ventures. The need to make profit may have resulted in Frobisher being given the liberty of the Fleet; in other words, for a fee, he could wander an area a mile and a half across beyond the prison walls. The Marshalsea stood in Southwark and there is no explanation given for Frobisher's transfer there. Again, there was surprising freedom for wealthy prisoners, most of whom were known to be anti-authoritarian.

By March 1570, Frobisher was once again in circulation, on the payment of a £900 fine, which had been made possible through the advocacy of the Lord Admiral, Edward de Clinton, and his wife, Elizabeth. William Cecil, the Queen's right-hand man, had also personally intervened to have him freed.

As was to be expected in the dog-eat-dog politics of Elizabeth's reign, Frobisher's release had various conditions attached. By 1571 he was in command of a small fleet tasked with intercepting pirates. It hardly squares with Frobisher's ability as a military naval commander that he failed to capture a single ship. In many ways, the politics of the time suited a slippery customer like Frobisher extremely well.

By this time tension between England and Spain had escalated. Pope Pius V had excommunicated Elizabeth for her treatment of Catholics and Philip sought to exploit any potential chinks in England's armour short of out and out war. The best way to do this was to support the continual insurrections in Ireland. The clans here were particularly susceptible to Spanish aid if it gave them the ability to fight a rival group. With no standing army, the Queen had considerable difficulty in containing this situation. Ireland had never fully been under English rule, and Elizabeth's excommunication had further alienated Ireland's largely Catholic population.

Philip was very aware of Ireland's simmering resentment and during the last three decades of the sixteenth century added to Elizabeth's worries by sending over 600 troops in support of Irish rebellion. This marked a continued need for a policy of plantation, in effect, English and Scottish subjects settling in

Ireland, as the local population's allegiances were uncertain. Gerald Fitzgerald, the Earl of Desmond, had been causing many problems in Ireland. Through infighting with his rivals and snubbing the English Court, he had been forced to give his lands up to the Queen and was imprisoned in the Tower, firstly in 1562, then again in 1566. In 1572, he attempted to employ Martin Frobisher to smuggle him and his brother out of London, back to Ireland. With Frobisher's uncle's links with the Mint, he almost certainly knew the layout of the building very well. The plan was thwarted and Desmond did not return to Ireland until the following year. This was hardly surprising. In 1571, the Queen herself had commissioned Frobisher to help subjugate uprisings in Ireland, but information on this is scant, underlining the secrecy of his mission. As so often in Elizabethan *realpolitik*, there is no paper trail. All this could be seen as part of a deliberate policy to Anglicize Ireland. In December of that year, bards, who traditionally sang songs about Irish history, were banned from performing. In Munster, the new president, Sir John Perrot, demanded that Irishmen cut their hair and beards and no longer wear 'Irish coats or great shirts' on pain of a £100 fine.

It was in Ireland that Frobisher met and served under Sir Humphrey Gilbert, his long-time friend and supporter of his upcoming voyages. As well as this, they had become involved in the rising orchestrated by James Fitzmaurice Fitzgerald. He was Desmond's cousin and had made repeated attacks on the power held by the English lieutenant, Henry Sidney. In reprisal, Sidney had seized Desmond's lands. When Fitzgerald burned the town of Kilmallock, Sidney was recalled to London in disgrace.

Frobisher's flair for espionage is revealed on two more occasions in this decade. Elizabeth's state was vulnerable, with potential attacks from without and within. It was as well for her that the man entrusted with state security was Francis Walsingham, a quietly fanatical Protestant with a shrewd and cunning turn of mind. He had risen under the auspices of

Lord Burghley, the Queen's chief minister and was the country's ambassador to France when Frobisher was in Ireland. He actually witnessed in Paris on St Bartholomew's Day the murder of an estimated 40,000 Protestants by Catherine de Medici's government, and returned to England to be made Secretary of State and elevated to the Privy Council. Walsingham was a brilliant spymaster but essentially he inherited a slow and clumsy system from his predecessors. Agents based abroad in reputable posts fed back to the Queen's government any scrap of information they could, to be assessed by the Privy Council. Thomas Jefferies operated out of Paris and Stephen Paule from Venice. Elsewhere, seven such men worked in the troubled Netherlands, thirteen throughout France, five in the Italian states and Spain and nine across the German states.

Some of these men were code-breakers, intercepting vital messages between foreign agents. Others were projectors, whose job it was to infiltrate conspiracies. There is no hard evidence for it, but it is conceivable that Martin Frobisher fulfilled this role. He had met the Queen and was a confidante of Henry Sidney, so he was ideally placed. If he was not operating at this level, he may have been an intelligencer, one who listened at keyholes, got men drunk and passed on tittle-tattle. This is light years away from the glossy heroism of a fictional James Bond, but the work was dangerous and, in keeping England safe from Irish rebellion, vital.

In 1573, when a number of Catholic agents entrusted Frobisher with the task of returning them to Spain, the ship they were on was captured before it even left London. A Spanish ambassador approached Frobisher to undertake what would have been a traitorous task on behalf of the King of Spain. It is by no means certain why Frobisher should have been selected. Perhaps his even-handed dealing with Protestant and Catholic pirate shipping made the Spaniards believe he was a man with whom they could do business. The plan was that Frobisher would lead a task force of English mercenaries to take Flushing (modern-day Vlissingen) for Spain. This ragtail army had just failed to relieve La Rochelle and it was very unlikely to succeed in this latest venture. Flushing was important as a strategic port in the escalation of tension between Dutch nationalists and their Spanish overlords. The plot was foiled, almost certainly because Frobisher was working as a double agent on behalf of Elizabeth's Privy Council.

Also in 1573, the Privy Council employed Frobisher in a plot to kidnap the English Catholic rebel Sir Thomas Stukeley. Stukeley was a soldier of fortune who had spent some time in the Tower of London for debt and was also implicated in treason on behalf of the French. Like Frobisher, he appeared before the Council on a charge of piracy and led a highly dubious lifestyle as the Captain of Berwick. This town on the border of Scotland had a reputation for duplicity. It had extremely strong defences and the Captain who controlled it was therefore in a strong position to make life difficult for the English government. Claiming that he was the illegitimate son of Henry VIII, he referred openly to the Queen as 'our dearest sister' and persistently escaped custody despite considerable evidence that he was involved in rebellion against her. In 1571, he became a hero in command of a squadron in the naval Battle of Lepanto against the Turks and was involved in a plot to invade England. When all this came to nothing, it was obvious that Frobisher's services would not be needed, but by this time he was unemployed and, as has been shown, had acquired a rather unenviable reputation for double-dealing.

It is clear, therefore, that a further facet to Frobisher's character and career was that of double agent. What did he use his time in Lisbon and West Africa doing? Was he endearing himself to the Spanish and Portuguese? Had he agreed to return home to England as a spy, only to turn double agent when he got there? At this point in his life Frobisher really does fit the image of a swashbuckling romantic – voyager, prisoner, pirate, soldier, spy. However, this chapter of his life was over almost as soon as it had begun. It could be that, as he had become too well known to remain a privateer, the same was true of him as a spy. Perhaps these exploits were not sufficiently daring for a man who, as his uncle described him, was of 'great spirit and bould courage, and naturall hardnes of body'. His thoughts returned to a project that he had first considered almost twenty years earlier, a route to the Orient, avoiding the perils of the Cape of Good Hope[5] and the long landlocked, heavily taxed overland routes through dangerous Tartar country and the Russian Steppes, a route by sea, a new route, the North-West Passage?

Chapter 3

North, South, East or West: The Quest for Asia

For 3,000 years commercial and cultural links had existed from the Mediterranean to the Far East, by land and by sea. The land route became known as the Silk Road; a vast network of trade routes, which saw civilizations from ancient Egypt, Rome, Greece and Persia to later peoples like the Moors, Saracens and Mongols exchanging highly prized commodities such as gold, silver, spices and textiles. It dictated patterns of conquest, and focused centres of power. But by the 1400s, because of repeated attacks by Arabs, such trade had declined to a trickle.

Shifting power bases and increasingly sedentary civilizations meant that markets were becoming more localized. The bubonic plague had swept along the Silk Road in the 1340s, killing at least a third of the world's population. In Europe, trade had become maritime based and more focused on the West. The only real way to obtain Asian spices was via the Venetian merchants operating out of Egypt and Constantinople. Once this city fell to the Ottoman Turks in the summer of 1453, even this outlet was closed. It was a sellers' market and the Venetians had long been used to exploiting their monopolies in the Eastern Mediterranean – as with any minority controlling a commodity, this did not come cheaply. China and India were vastly advanced producing nations. They were able to manufacture goods in greater numbers, more cheaply and to a higher standard than their Western counterparts; silk and porcelain in China, and cotton textiles in India. These markets were hugely attractive to European trade, but with limited access to them, it was necessary to look for alternatives. One way to do this was to establish bases in both of those countries. To that end, the East India Company was founded in London in 1600 and began to set up trading posts on the Indian coast. The French Compagnie des Indes was doing the same thing at the same time. The other means of competing was for European countries to produce their own goods, but the climate was not conducive to cotton growing in Western Europe and it would be 300 years before entrepreneurs like Josiah Wedgwood were able to produce 'home grown' copies of porcelain.

Many voyages to South and North America were also initially undertaken to try to find a route to the Orient, sometimes erroneously identified as being part of the Americas. The most famous example is of course that of Cristoforo Colon (Columbus), who continued to believe, despite obvious evidence to the contrary, that when he found Hispaniola in 1492, he had actually located India. His christening of the Arawak natives 'Indians' has become something of an offensive word today. In 1488, Bartolommeo Diaz reached the very tip of South Africa, the Cape of Good Hope. Less than a decade later, Vasco da Gama had successfully rounded the Cape and reached India. He was followed by Pedro Cabral, who took such a westward sweep to circumnavigate the Cape that he inadvertently discovered Brazil.

Although the Asian markets were far from open to European traders at this point, by 1511 the Portuguese had been able to establish control of the significant trading centre of Malacca in Malaya, and also conducted trade in Cochin, Cambodia and Goa, India. This was through a combination of threat and conflict (the Europeans were the first to conduct armed trade in Asia) and also a calculated avoidance of involvement in local politics. The numerous independent kingdoms were often very divided by war. However, in evading the latter Portugal was never fully able to control trade in the whole of Asia. Later colonists, particularly the British and French, had no qualms about using force to protect their trading interests in areas that came under their sway.

From Cochin and Malacca, the Portuguese pushed on into the South China Seas, where by 1517 they had established trade in Guangzhou and territory in Macao in Southern China. Into the 1520s they were able to exploit a trade ban between China and Japan, exchanging plentiful Japanese silver for desirable Chinese silk.

Of all nations that could have contested Portuguese expansion and power it was, perhaps ironically, the Chinese that did. In the early fifteenth century, Cheng Ho and Admiral Zheng He commanded vast fleets that controlled the Indian Ocean, the China Seas and reached the coast of East Africa. Had they felt it necessary, they were also more than capable of rounding the Cape of Good Hope, as they possessed greater technological, meteorological and navigational skills than their European counterparts, and the sheer size of the fleets would also have made them a formidable force to be reckoned with. However, by the 1420s the Ming Dynasty, finding these expeditions expensive, brought the fleet back to home waters. China controlled many of the smaller states that surrounded it and these were obliged to pay tribute to the Chinese, so a need to expand markets was of arguable importance. Additionally, the Chinese did not do things by halves, the trading fleets comprising hundreds of vessels, as opposed to the maximum tens of Europe, so the cost factor was hugely significant. Whilst the Portuguese made use of their bases in Africa, the rest of Europe sought other new and hopefully better routes to Asia.

Between 1492 and 1504, Columbus's four voyages to the West established the preferred route of the Spanish. Although his initial discoveries of Cuba and Hispaniola were incorrectly identified by some as a peninsula of China, the potential of this 'New World' was soon realized. He subsequently charted much of the West Indies and northern parts of South America. The Spanish conquistadores Francisco Hernandez de Cordoba (1517) and Alonso Alvarez Pineda (1519) continued to try and identify a route through the West Indies, finding it landlocked, but were more than happy to exploit the area and the Gulf of Mexico, creating an empire based largely on slavery and prompting the destruction of the rich Aztec and Incan civilizations. It was not until 1521 that Fernando Magellan and Juan Sebastian Elcano successfully rounded the tip of South America, reaching the Philippines and going on to complete the first circumnavigation of the globe. Magellan himself did not live to see it, and so gruelling was the voyage that of the 237 men who set out, only 18 completed the journey and managed to return to Spain.

For the English, French and Dutch, the route lay to the North. Since the ninth century, there had been exploration further west into the frozen lands of Iceland, Greenland, North America and Canada. The Vikings, one of the greatest seafaring and exploring peoples, began to establish colonies in the Arctic, such as Eiriksfjord, the homestead of Eric the Red, on the east coast of Greenland. The Viking Sagas, although intended to be entertainment sung around smoky fires in winter, are actually histories of such explorations. It is difficult to decipher the place names and relate them to the geography of what is known today. It was from Greenalnd, perhaps by accident, that Bjarni Herjoffson, blown off course, first sighted the coast of Labrador at the end of the tenth century. Eric the Red's own son Leif 'The Lucky' traced this course a few years later, landing and wintering in Vinland, or Newfoundland, at the end of the first millennium. About five years after this, Thorfinn Karlsefni settled there with a group of around a hundred would-be colonists, but the stretched supply routes from Greenland, coupled with repeated hostilities with the indigenous population, meant that this community only survived for a few years. By the late fourteenth century, the majority of settlements in the North had also been abandoned. A notoriously inhospitable climate meant that agriculture was unable to flourish. The situation was worsened by a cold snap between the thirteenth and fifteenth centuries, which has come to be known as the Little Ice Age. It is notable that when putting forward a case for travelling to the North-West in the sixteenth century, one of the primary arguments was that the land would be good for settlement and agriculture, a statement utterly refuted by the collapse of the Norse colonies. However, this period of civilization meant that the cod-rich waters around Greenland and North America were well known to fishermen and traders.

In the 1550s a map, known as the Zeno map, was published. It charted the voyages of the Venetian Zeno brothers, Nicolo and Antonio, in the late 1300s. It maps out parts of Greenland, the Shetland Isles and North America, as well as islands named Estland, Icaria, Frisland and Estotiland. It was accompanied by letters telling the tale of the brothers' voyages and their encounters with the local inhabitants. It came to be held in high regard by many well-thought-of cartographers, such as Gerardus Mercator, the greatest geographer of the age. But there was a problem. It was a hoax. The appearance of land masses that resembled Greenland and North America were tenuous, and the islands such as Estotiland and Icaria were totally fictitious. The map itself had been published by a descendant of the Zenos, the younger brother Nicolo's namesake, and appears merely to have been a glorification of their legacy. It is likely that fishermen's tales of the area also played a major part in the construction of the fantastical map and its accompanying history. The fact that it was accepted as accurate by so many of the 'experts' of the day shows how little was known of the North. In truth then, Europeans knew as little of the North as they did of the West and South, and discovery would simply be a case of trial and error. This was an age when the science of exploration was in its infancy, without clear notions of longitude; even the concept that the world was round was still a novel idea.

Perhaps the least skilled in these matters were the English. This was ironic bearing in mind the fact that England has always been a maritime nation. Various continental neighbours had more substantial overseas concerns during this period and certainly access to more significant amounts of revenue. In addition, greater minds were available to them, the Renaissance having originated in mainland Europe. There is no doubt that England was a backwater at this time. Henry VIII did his best to impress when he met Francis I at the Field of the Cloth of Gold in 1520, but the French king's wealth and power far surpassed Henry's. The Renaissance movement originated in Italy and only spread to England later. Therefore, it was not until the seventeenth century, in what has come to be known as the scientific revolution, that Englishman Isaac Newton could stand alongside the great philosophers of Europe; to some, in fact, he stood on the shoulders of giants.

The first expedition to the North to set out from England was not even led by an Englishman, although the cash and ships to equip the voyage were English. It was the notable Genoese pilot John Cabot who sailed from Bristol and reached Newfoundland in 1497. For France, Jacques Cartier had succeeded in penetrating the North American coast, and travelled up the St Lawrence River in 1534. But there was still no clear sign of a passage through, although some questioned whether either land mass encountered may have been the coast of China.

It was not only a passage North-West that was considered. With an embargo on trade through the Middle East, and the difficulties of navigation and the Portuguese threat to the South, the English also sought routes North-East.

So it was in 1553 that Sir Hugh Willoughby and Richard Chancellor set sail around the north of Scandinavia, down into modern-day Russia, known at the time as Muscovy. Both men were members of the verbose 'Mystery and Company of

Merchant Adventurers for the Discovery of Regions, Dominions, Islands, and Places Unknown', of which Michael Lok and John Yorke were also members. Willoughby's voyage was disastrous. Returning via Scandinavia, his ship became trapped in an ice floe and the entire crew froze to death, to be found some months later by Russian fishermen. Chancellor had more success, and entered the White Sea. His arrival in North Western Russia was brought to the attention of the monarch of the Muscovite empire, Ivan IV, the Terrible. The first man to use the title 'tsar', Ivan is often portrayed as a psychopathic monster who inflicted torture and death on thousands of his own subjects. He was also ambitious and interested in anyone, from East or West, who could enlarge his territory and increase his power.

From this point, an important trade and diplomatic relationship was realized, and the Muscovy Company was created in 1555. This may seem to have been a step forward. However, despite the discovery of a new route into Russia, there was also a need to conduct much travel on land. Chancellor himself had had to endure a 600-mile journey overland through ice and snow even to reach Ivan's court in Moscow. Also, the Muscovite ruler was unwilling to allow trade to progress East without receiving a considerable cut of the profits. So the Muscovy Company soon resumed their search for alternative routes to expand their markets. As there was no confirmed sighting of a North-West Passage, and previous expeditions had been of arguable commercial success, the merchants were not as ready to part with their money to finance further voyages. It was left to the theorists of the day, and those who had a passion, such as Martin Frobisher, to put forward the case for the existence of the passage, and it would take over twenty years to do so.

Chapter 4

The Case for the North–West Passage

*'the way is dangerous, the route doubtful, the voyage
not thoroughly known'*[1]
Richard Willes, 1575

Of all the potential routes to the markets of Asia, the one to the North–West was the most uncertain in terms of tangible evidence. Cartography at the time was basic at best and riddled with inaccuracies. In the nascent age of exploration, people relied heavily on tales and theories rather than actual evidence.

In 1573, William Bullein wrote an imaginary conversation in his *Dialogue Against the Pestilence* in which a traveller (Mendax) claimed to have seen the most wonderful sights. In the Isle of Rue, in the great Can's land, mermaids and fishes came out of the water and slept in the trees, fighting with the native apes. The humans were cannibals (only eating female flesh) and parrots played chess. In Selentide, women gave birth by laying eggs. The Scipodes had only one foot. Ippopodes had horse's hooves for feet. In Fanesii, men's ears were as long as cloaks and their city wall 400 miles long, the streets paved with gold. Men went naked, with two heads and six hands apiece.

Although this work was no doubt intended to entertain, it was based on exactly the sort of stories passed on by explorers themselves. When asked why he did not bring back some of the fabulous treasure he had found, Mendax had a plausible answer. His ship sailed near the adamant (magnetic) rocks and the whole lot was whisked overboard!

The Zeno brothers' map was based on mariners' tales and Humphrey Gilbert used the lost civilization of Atlantis to try and prove a route through the north of America to China. The *Theatrum Orbis Terrarum*, or World Map, by Flemish cartographer Abraham Ortelius was published in 1570. It showed an assumed passage along the North American coast, based on the small amount of knowledge of the coastline with its maze of inlets and riverways. Ortelius, born in Antwerp, was widely travelled in Europe. As much a businessman as map-maker, he produced the atlas under the auspices of his friend Mercator. His 1564 'mappemonde' was a more complex version of the *Orbis Terrarum* and only one copy of it exists today.

The celebrated geographer Gemma Frisius produced a globe in 1534, which showed a peninsula of China hanging over the north of North America separated by a passage of water. Frisius was born Jemme Reinersz of poor parents in Friesland. As a medical student at Leuven university, he became fascinated by mathematics and set up a workshop for the making of globes. The system of triangulation he devised in 1533 is still in use in surveying today. Twenty years later, he was working on a clock to determine longitude, prompting the famous comment by Jean-Baptiste Morin: 'I do not know if the Devil will succeed in making a longitude timekeeper but it is folly for man to try.' Published in 1568, André Thevet's book on Antarctica and the New World says little of what lay to the north of North America, at least honest about the flaws in the available evidence. Thevet hailed from Augoulême and was a Franciscan priest with an exploratory bent. He visited Brazil but the work relevant to this book was *Singularitez de la France Antarctique*, relating essentially to the area around Rio de Janeiro.

At this time there was no universal method of navigation or map-making, as theories were still being postulated and new discoveries being made. The science of navigation and cartography itself was too new to be wholly accurate. For example, few if any at the time knew how to plot accurately lines of longitude. Maps were almost always presented in plane rather than round, and longitudinal lines were placed equidistant and in line with the Equator, meaning that the further east or west on a map, the more distorted the actual position of landmasses appeared. It was best for a sailor simply to plot a course and stick to it, hoping there was not land in the way, or if there was, believing it to be the desired destination, as in the case of Columbus. It would only be through further exploration and developments in science that these problems could be addressed. Beyond this, one had to find the means to get to sea in the first place. Maps and navigational tools were, despite their shortcomings, very expensive, as were supplies, crews and, of course, the ships to carry them.

It has been suggested that Frobisher's interest in the North-West dates back to his time in Lisbon, and then upon studying charts in the 1560s. If true, his likely motivation is beautifully summed up by George Best, who interviewed Frobisher on his voyages: '(Frobisher knew) this to be the only thing of the world . . . left undone whereby a notable mind mighte be made famous and fortunate.'[2] This certainly rings true of the former privateer who was keen to advance himself financially and gain patronage, and also pertains to his career as a soldier and sailor, which saw him knighted, first by the Lord Admiral, Howard of Effingham, and then by the Queen. This then is merely the 'next stage' in the life of a man who doubtless missed the life of privilege he had been sent from some thirty years previously. But Frobisher could not undertake this alone; he needed the help of the friends and patrons his colourful life had thus far afforded him.

Sir Humphrey Gilbert was a sailor like Frobisher, and shared his love of fame and fortune, although he also harboured a true desire for discovery and was an articulate and educated man. Perhaps slightly overshadowed by his younger half-brother, Sir Walter Ralegh, 'that great Lucifer', Gilbert had been heavily involved in the suppression of the Irish rebellions, where he is likely to have met Martin Frobisher.

The two men were of an age, and Gilbert, the Oxford-educated son of a landowning Dartmouth family, would have been drawn to the well-travelled Frobisher. In fact, their involvement in the settling of English communities in Ireland in an attempt to pacify the local Irish populations may well have further sparked his interest in colonization. As an educated gentleman, Gilbert used contemporary and historical sources to put forward his case for a passage to the North-West. Using Plato, Pliny, Philo and contemporaries such as Gemma Frisius and Mercator, Gilbert put forward his arguments in *A Discourse of a Discoverie for a New Passage to Cataia*.

No educated man in the sixteenth century moved far intellectually without consulting the ancients. The whole thrust of the Renaissance through which Frobisher and Gilbert lived was backward-looking, attempting to recreate the 'glory that was Greece and the grandeur that was Rome' and there was an automatic assumption that the ancient scholars knew best. Plato was the greatest of the Greek philosophers whose ideas were in some ways the cornerstone of European society. Pliny (the Elder) was a first-century writer on natural history, compiling seventy-seven volumes of his *Historia Naturalis* with comments on everything he saw about him. Philo was a second-century Byzantine scholar whose work on what today would be termed physics has only survived in fragments.

Written in 1566, Gilbert's *Discourse* was not published until 1576 in promotion of Frobisher's voyages, but it did help to raise awareness and interest in the potential of such a venture prior to publication. His treatise begins with Plato's writings on Atlantis, the fabled land that was supposedly destroyed by floods and earthquakes. As it is stated that Atlantis was an island, beyond the Pillars of Hercules (the Strait of Gibraltar), Gilbert suggested that America and Greenland were what remained of Atlantis, separated from China and each other by the earthquakes that had decimated it: 'The Northwest . . .

swallowed up with water . . . be on occasion of the enlarging of the olde, and also an inforcing of a great many new, why then should we now doubt of our Northwest passage . . . From England to India?'[3] As well as contemporary geographers, those who had travelled far enough were similarly convinced of the passage. In 1497, Cabot stated that had bad weather (and a disgruntled crew) not forced his return from Newfoundland, he would have headed straight into such a pathway. As the first pilot of England under Elizabeth's grandfather Henry VII, this would have been a compelling statement to use regardless of its foundation in an age where position and reputation counted for more than accuracy and truth: 'All which learned men . . . have affirmed . . . that America was an Island and that there lyeth a great sea between it, Cataia and Grondland, by the which any man of our country (could) passe to Cataia, the Moluccae, India and all places in the East.'[4]

Where most of Gilbert's supporting statements were tenuous, others were farcical, none more so than his use of Pliny's translations of the twelfth century. He writes of a group of fishermen, Asian in appearance who landed in Germany having been blown off course in a storm. The fact is that, if this story is true, they are far more likely to have come from the East. Perhaps they were circumpolar Celts from around Siberia or the Middle East, and their wide-featured, dark-skinned, dark-haired appearance would have been juxtaposed by the fair skinned Celts of mainland Europe. Gilbert seems to have ignored this. He insists they can only have come from the North-West due to the nature of their ships and the oceanic currents. This does not simply display a lack of knowledge, but underlines how stories were used to suit a purpose. Gilbert's most intelligent and compelling argument was that if no navigable passage exists, why then are there no animals or peoples from Asia living in America? This is, however, based on the supposition that the landmass to the north of North America was in fact China rather than Canada.

Gilbert was not unopposed in his theories in England. Anthony Jenkinson, a member of the Muscovy Company, believed, as his company's founders had, that a better route lay to the North-East. He supported his argument with Tartarian tales of unimpeded voyages south, and the discovery of unicorn horns, equally spurious arguments, particularly considering the fate of Willoughby and the arduous journey to Moscow of his partner Chancellor. Jenkinson himself had undertaken an abortive eight-month journey over land and across rivers and had been halted at modern-day Uzbekistan in 1563. Gilbert countered that Tartars were not able enough sailors to undertake such a voyage, and that unicorns did not exist on the Asian continent and that it was more likely elephant ivory. This obsession with mythical beasts comes from the reliance on sailors' tall tales and 'unicorn horns' also feature in accounts of Frobisher's voyages, on these occasions turning out to be narwhal tusks. There is a very clear distinction between half-seen, half-forgotten real animals – rhinoceroses and oryx could well have been taken for unicorns – and downright fabrication (mermaids, for instance) in these tall tales.

Clearly, Gilbert could not rely on history alone and needed to expound the virtues of the new route and potential for settlement and economic gain. This new route would be much faster than the existing overland routes monopolized by Spain and Portugal. This would have become an increasingly attractive prospect after 1570 when tensions between England and her Catholic neighbours began to spiral. He was also keen to highlight the benefits of colonization: 'We might inhabit some parte of those countreys . . . and settle there such needie people of our countrie, which now trouble the common welth, and through want here at home, are inforced to commit outrageous offences . . .'.[5] This is a very progressive idea, one that became extensively employed in Australia in the nineteenth century. Richard Hakluyt, a lecturer in geography at Oxford and writer of the greatest travelogue of the age, *The Principall Navigations, Voyages, Traffiques and Discoveries of the*

English Nation (1598–1600), was a huge supporter of Gilbert's socio-economic ideas. He too was keen to promote expansion into the New World and used Gilbert's writings as a blueprint, quoting him extensively. He recognized the need to establish settlements and a supply base and suggested that the New World had a climate perfect for this. However, neither Hakluyt nor Gilbert had ever set foot in the New World, let alone its northern extremes. Reports on climate were based on those from no further north than Newfoundland, where it is not dissimilar to Europe; they had no comprehension of the savage winters that existed north of Baffin Bay. Most voyages and attempts to settle in the North had failed. The Vikings in Greenland had been forced to leave a century and a half earlier due to the privations of winter and an inability to sustain agriculture; they had only lasted a matter of years in North America. The Elizabethan adventurer would learn from his own mistakes it would seem, but not those of history; why had no one successfully travelled and found a North-West passage? Why were settlements not already in existence or had been abandoned? Whether this was adventurous optimism or blind ignorance, it is not possible to say, but it would take the best part of a century before any kind of recognizable and sustainable civilization could be established in North America and Canada.

Despite its myriad inconsistencies and blind suppositions to a modern eye, Gilbert's *Discourse* was to prove important in raising awareness of the possibility of a passage to the North-West. An enthusiastic and well-connected individual who had been a member of Elizabeth's court for a decade, he was if nothing else an able promoter. In 1565 he tried to gain the patronage of the Queen. Notoriously tight-fisted, she did not give it, but instead suggested Gilbert go straight to the Muscovy Company to ask them. As the Pope had granted a monopoly to the Spaniards and Portuguese in Africa, so had the Muscovy Company's charter afforded them similar control of all routes North, and a voyage of this nature could not be undertaken without a licence from them. Whether Elizabeth merely did not see any merit in Gilbert's plan, or that she had been inundated with requests in court that day, is unclear. Certainly the Queen had her hands full that summer with the disturbing news that her Catholic cousin, Mary, Queen of Scots, had married Henry Stuart, Lord Darnley, who had a claim to the English throne. The Muscovy Company was still consolidating its new markets in Russia and perhaps suspicious or protective of opening up a new venture to an outside party and consequently refused Gilbert's application. But it must have been worrying to the company that in November the Flemish navigator Olivier Brunels was exploring the White Sea, establishing a Dutch trading post at Archangel on the delta of the Dvina River.

Like Gilbert, Frobisher had previously tried and failed to gain a licence from the Muscovy Company. In George Best's account of the voyages, he writes of how Frobisher was incensed by the Muscovy Company's greed, which overrode any desire to push further into unknown lands. This is ironic, as his motivation was as financial as theirs. Frobisher would need more powerful men than Gilbert to help his cause. He found these in the form of William Cecil, Lord Burghley, Elizabeth's right-hand man and future Lord Treasurer and brothers Ambrose Dudley, Earl of Warwick and Robert Dudley, Earl of Leicester, Master of the Horse and favourite of the Queen.

Elizabeth was known to have surrounded herself with loyal and doting male subjects. Flirtation was as important as fealty, and although she never married, her lovers were numerous. Robert Dudley, nicknamed 'Eyes' by Elizabeth, was rarely far from her side. On the death of his wife in 1563 he even became a contender for the Queen's hand, although in reality this would never have happened as the political ramifications were insurmountable. Rumours abounded of their love affair but they were hushed rumours as the quick-tempered Queen was known to imprison those who commented on her private life.

William Cecil, though not romantically involved with the Queen, was her most trusted advisor, and similarly rarely left her side. By persuading these men of the merits of his venture, Frobisher had both ears of the Queen. So it was that Martin succeeded in convincing these powerful men of the financial, territorial and political benefits that such a voyage could deliver, and in 1574 William Cecil wrote to the Muscovy Company in support of Frobisher. He was given another audience but the merchants were still reluctant to grant him a licence. In the meantime, Warwick, a member of the Privy Council, had begun to champion Frobisher's cause, writing a letter with fellow council members in 1575. By the end of January the licence had been issued.

There was another key player in ensuring that Frobisher was heard, though not perhaps as much as he would like history to think. It is a name from Frobisher's past, the name of Lok. Michael Lok was a member of the Muscovy Company and brother to John, who had led the expedition to Guinea where the young Frobisher had been left as a hostage in the hands of the Portuguese. A gifted financier, it is fortunate that through him there are fastidious records of all expenditures and debts for the voyages, although this would ultimately lead to his undoing after what was financially a disastrous undertaking. In Lok's own account, which amounts to a slim autobiography, he says: 'And of late by God's good providence renewing my old acquaintance with Martin Frobisher, gentleman and finding him sufficient and ready to execute the attempt of so great matters, I joined with him and to my power advanced him to the world with credit . . . to the intent the whole world might be opened unto England.'[6] Michael saw the potential for profit in the expedition, coupled with the high-profile patrons that Frobisher had amassed, and he pushed the licence through. It is unlikely that any personal consideration came into his thoughts, particularly in light of the fact that his brother had abandoned Frobisher to an unknown fate in Guinea, and that Frobisher had twice failed to gain a licence from a committee that Lok sat on. However, from the moment the licence was granted, the two men were essentially partners. Lok even resigned his position with the company to focus entirely on this endeavour. This relationship would not be a long standing one, but Lok's involvement was crucial.

The licence was only half the battle, however. The ships, crew and supplies all still needed to be secured, and with a man like Frobisher at the helm, this would not be easy. A convicted thief and known privateer, Frobisher found no one at court willing to invest in his expedition. Lok opened up opportunities on a sliding scale of investment to try to entice gentleman–adventurers and fellow merchants to invest, but none took the bait. It was a further year before the funds could be raised.

This happened for a number of reasons. Lok, aware of Frobisher's bad credit, employed a purser to control the finances whilst at sea. He also employed two ship's masters, Christopher Hall, a talented navigator from Limehouse, and Owen Griffyne. This was to draw focus away from Frobisher as commander and convince investors that their money would be safe. Slowly, the coffers began to swell. Burghley, Leicester and Warwick all invested £50. Other courtiers, including Sir Francis Walsingham, Elizabeth's spy master, invested £25. This was an interesting move. Walsingham was in charge of English espionage and may or may not have been Frobisher's employer during his dealings with the Spanish. Whatever his relationship with Frobisher, Walsingham would certainly have been aware of him; a man like Walsingham knew everything and everyone. Was he investing in the career of an able and adept spy, or was he investing in a venture that would be a thorn in the side of Spain? Lok, Sir Thomas Gresham, William Bond and William Burde, associates of Lok, each put in the majority share of £100. Gresham was the foremost financier of his day and to have a man with his reputation involved was important. He founded the Royal Exchange and became a royal servant, living in what was virtually a palace at

Bishopsgate, London, and owned a number of country houses. His grasshopper crest can be still found in use in London's banking community.

William Bond was an alderman of the City of London and sometime Sheriff, sharing with William Burde the career of merchant adventurer. A total of eighteen investors put in nearly £900 to get the expedition off the ground. It is unwise to draw modern parallels as so many other factors must be taken into account such as cost of living, the value of gold, national income etc. However, Robert Ruby, in his *Unknown Shores*, suggests as a bench mark that any amount should be multiplied by a factor of 400 to approach a modern equivalent, meaning the total investment reached £350,000 by today's reckoning. And what did the investors get in return? Burghley, Warwick and Leicester almost certainly struck a deal with Frobisher when they originally championed his cause, so their potential share is open to argument. For the main part, those who invested £100 were to receive 100,000 acres of land with full baronial rights, after the second voyage, and the discovery of ore, which was extended to all precious metals on the land. For £50 investors could expect 1,000 acres, and for anything under that, 500 acres. Anyone travelling at their own expense was entitled to a third of what they found.

Lok was disappointed with the amount and put up almost the same amount again, £738 of his own money, to ensure that the voyage would be sufficiently provisioned. With money invested, the preparations could begin. Books, charts and navigational apparatus were obtained with no expense spared, despite the fact that not all of them were necessary purchases. Thomas Hackett's translation of Thevet's book showed little information north of Newfoundland. Probably the most useful publication, Pedro de Medina's *Regimento de Navegacio* had yet to be translated into English so was of even less worth. Mercator's world map of 1569 was purchased, showing a clear if inaccurate route similar to that of Ortelius' map of 1570, which was also bought. Perhaps most needless of all, and at a cost of £50, was a skeletal map of what little was known about the coastline created by navigator and supplier of ships for voyage three, William Borough. It exists in facsimile form in the British library and is an A3 sized chart with half of the English coast, a little of Greenland and a random unmarked inlet. Hall actually used this chart to make new additions as it was such a blank canvas, which was of more use than the original, and indeed led towards the revisiting of methods relating to longitude.

Two globes were purchased, one to plot navigation, the other a celestial orb, though both were probably too advanced to be used to their full advantage. In this period, astronomy was as important as science; a sailor could always find and follow the North Star. An early theodolite, the *holometrum geometrum*, was also acquired to plot coastlines. The most important tools to an everyday sailor, however, were the ship's compasses, hourglasses, to plot time and position, and the simple cross staff, which could be used to calculate altitude against the sun by day and the North Star by night. These charts and texts, and the more complex instruments were more likely to inform before the voyage set sail than they were to be used at sea. And with such complex theories, coupled with the relative inexperience of Frobisher and Hall, it was necessary to bring in an expert in the latest notions of navigation. Enter the notable astronomer, mathematician, geographer and magician, the most celebrated mind of Elizabethan England, Dr John Dee.

Dee was educated at Cambridge and had studied under the two prominent geographers of the age, Gemma Frisius and Mercator. In 1553 he had been commissioned by the Muscovy Company to help produce cosmographical charts for their North-East expeditions. A tutor to Robert Dudley, he was astrologer and philosopher to Elizabeth herself at a time when there was a Europe-wide fascination with almanacs, kalendars and prognostications. He owned probably the largest library at the time, which contained over 4,000 publications, and 2 laboratories, in which he conducted his experiments. In

1570 he invented two compasses, the Paradoxall compass and the compass of variation. The latter was used on Frobisher's voyages, as it always maintained True North and could be used to ensure that standard compasses did not deviate and therefore adjustments could be made. In the year that Frobisher sailed, an Englishman named Robert Norman discovered the magnetic 'dip' in a compass needle caused by the earth's magnetic field not running exactly parallel to its surface.

Although Dee was associated with alchemy, the black arts and the sinister School of Night, a pseudo-scientific group that attracted dangerous men like Walter Ralegh, the 'Wizard Earl' Northumberland and the mathematician Thomas Heriot, his mathematical and scientific brain was much in demand and he was supported by the Crown in his Mortlake residence. He was to tutor Lok, a fellow enthusiast of navigational techniques, and Hall and Frobisher in geometry and trigonometry to help in plotting navigational routes. He agreed, perhaps as his tutor Mercator had displayed it, that there was a certain passage to the North-West. How much of their teachings Frobisher and Hall took with them is arguable, but it does show that every opportunity was extended to them in this venture.

Three ships were commissioned, although the original plan had been to equip one large vessel. Perhaps the smaller ships would be better able to cope with the icy waters and narrow routes that would be encountered, but the reason was more likely to have been financial. The *Gabriel* and its accompanying pinnace, a smaller vessel used to conduct expeditions inland or carry men ashore, were built for purpose. The *Michael* was purchased for £120. These vessels would not have been dissimilar in size, at about 50ft, to those used by the Vikings over the previous few centuries, although their three masts and complex rigging would have set them apart from their Norse precursors.

The records of the voyages of Martin Frobisher are the most complete of any sixteenth-century merchant venture and the expenses for the equipment for this trip survive. The bill for maps and nautical instruments amounted to £51 1s 6d, the single most-expensive item for a 'greate globe of metal in blanke in a case' at £7 13s 4d. They took twenty different types of compass, eighteen hourglasses for keeping time, an astrolabe and copies of books by Thevet and Mercator. The fact that they bought a new Bible (for £1) showed that they were not trusting to navigational science alone. They also bought a copy of Sir John Mandeville's voyages of discovery, a fourteenth-century text cataloguing travels to India and the East.[7]

The ships' medical chests contained forty different drugs, including aloes, myrrh, cardamom, lapis lazuli, borax and camphor.

The individual items, mostly paid for by Michael Lok, included luxuries for the officers. Frobisher was paid 10 guineas for out-of-purse expenses and his ship's bed cost £3 16s 5d. The cost of the launch party for the *Gabriel* ran to 19s (mostly for bread and beer). Pans of brass and iron make up the lists of the inventory along with wooden platters and pewter ewers. The men's wages amounted to £213 17s (over the odds in comparison with the average journey) and the ammunition for the ships' guns to £172 3s 6d.

The crew consisted of thirty-four men, eighteen aboard the *Gabriel*, including Frobisher and Hall, and seventeen aboard the *Michael*, captained by Griffyne. Of the skilled hands aboard there were two gunners, a carpenter and smith, a surgeon and a cooper, the rest made of assorted sailors including a first mate and a boatswain. Paying the men well was likely to ensure that Lok and his fellow investors' interests were more secure and would safeguard potential profit. The supply cargo included about 1,300lb of rice, 1,100lb of butter, 220lb of cheese, 11 oxen, 8,000lb of the dreaded weevil-infested ships biscuit and over 1,135 gallons of wine and beer, most of which would spoil, save salted fish and meat. This meant that a 'balanced diet' at sea consisted of only 8oz of cereal against a gallon of beer. It was generally believed that Elizabethan sailors would tolerate *any* conditions, no matter how appalling, as long as the beer supply was plentiful.

The two ships set sail from their Ratcliff mooring on 7 June 1576, three months behind schedule. They had to put into port almost immediately at Deptford (3 miles away) as the pinnace had been damaged travelling along the Thames. They left Deptford on the following day, and saluted the royal palace – Placentia – at Greenwich along the way. Elizabeth is said to have sent an envoy out to the boats to wish them well. They reached the mouth of the Thames on 12 June, and turned North.

Chapter 5

The First Voyage

The ships, now in open waters, were dogged by turbulent seas, and before passing northern Scotland they once again had to put into port to carry out repairs, as the *Michael* had sprung a leak. They moored in the Shetland Isles, and before setting off had to redefine their course. Even for hardened sailors, this journey was to be a rough one. The Shetland Isles, with their craggy coasts and safe harbours few and far between, were gentle compared with what was to come. Frobisher wished to be close to 60° north before turning the course westward. Hall as pilot master would have undertaken this through use of the cross staff. This was an awkward and arduous task, as the staff had to be held at eye level for long enough for a reading to be taken. Rough seas and a pitching ship would require numerous measurements to be taken, with the added risk of being blinded by the sun while taking readings. This made Hall's job as arduous as any mariner aboard. Before leaving their Shetland port, the two wrote to their tutor, John Dee, thanking him for his teachings but lamenting they had not been better pupils, his 'poor disciples'. Now they were on their own.

They were afforded a few days grace in calm waters and, finding azure seas, whales and seabirds circling overhead, they sent out the pinnace to fish. This was an important supplement to their diet, particularly as the cereal and dairy supplies would soon spoil. During the first week of July, the weather began to turn, blue skies became grey, then black, fog descended and the seas were whipped into a frenzy. The ensuing gale blew for a week. The sails of the ships were stripped and the crews were at the mercy of the waves, clinging on for dear life. The fate of the pinnace was sealed in these tumultuous waters. Loose of its mooring to one of the larger ships it was lost from sight in the fog and the swelling seas claimed it and the lives of those aboard; no sign of them remained. Fortunately for the *Michael* and *Gabriel*, shortly after the pinnace was lost, the storms abated, and three days later at 61° latitude the *Gabriel* sighted land.

Hall writes: 'we had sight of the land of Friseland . . . west northwest . . . and rising like pinnacles of steeples and covered with snow'.[1] It is fortunate that Hall kept a detailed log of the course of the voyage. Although he limits this to simple observation and recording, rather than the more colourful writing of Best, for example, it is possible to follow the course of the voyage. Friseland was one of the fictitious islands taken from the Zeno brothers' voyages and adopted by Mercator in his world map. From Hall's readings, however, we can see that they had in fact reached the east coast of Greenland, which was hugely misplaced far to the north in maps of the day. On passing this coast on the final voyage in 1578, Hall draws Greenland's mountainous east coast in his log and affectionately names a series of needle-like peaks after his mentor, 'Mr Dee, his Pinnacles'. A breathtaking sight to any sailor, even those who had sailed north-east to reach Moscow, the huge glaciers and ice floes made this an incredibly dangerous part of the Atlantic to be in. The huge blocks of ice, calved from the glaciers ahead and so gleaming white as to appear blue, would have towered over the little ships. It is an even more treacherous stretch of water in summer months as the ice melts and flows swiftly via the eastern currents into the sea. A modern steel-hulled ship would need to be cautious in such conditions, but in a wooden hulled ship it would be suicidal to attempt to move further inland towards the ice. The *Michael* had become separated from the *Gabriel* and the pinnace during the previous storm. Though her crew also sighted Greenland, the fact that this was the first stage of the journey, coupled with the loss, they thought, of both the pinnace and the *Gabriel* and having been ravaged by storms, the prospect of the icy journey into the unknown was too much. They turned their course homeward and arrived back in London, according to Lok, on 'the first day of September'.

As will be seen later, there were faint hearts on campaigns like the Armada, but in a war situation, with national pride at stake and several friendly ships within hailing distance, the pressure was on to stay put, cope with the problem and hope for the best. But the *Michael* was on a peacetime mission into the unknown, in the uncharted waters of the mountainous North Atlantic and the temptation to cut and run had become paramount. It was the nightmare of all early explorers – how to keep frightened men loyal and on task in the face of despair.

The adventurous Frobisher and skilled Hall were not to be put off so easily. Realizing it was fruitless and dangerous to head inland, they made for open water. Mother Nature did not reward their determination, however, and that night she pummelled the *Gabriel* with a storm so fierce it nearly destroyed the ship. With sails torn, rigging decimated and the hold flooding, the ship was cast onto its side. The precious cargo of trinkets, buttons, bells and pocket knives, intended as trading items for the Eastern markets, were swept out to sea. The sea loomed black and forbidding, the *Gabriel* a feather caught by a typhoon. The most startling imagery from paintings and footage of seas caught in the grip of hurricanes cannot give us even a glimpse of the horror that filled every man's heart aboard the craft, a fraction of the size of Columbus' smallest vessel. Now on its side, the crew must have thought this was the end. Now was the time for Frobisher to show his mettle. He was a hardened mariner and a man of great strength, as his relations and friends were quick to relate. From somewhere deep within, he summoned the courage and strength to cut free the mizzen mast, preventing the sail from forcing the ship further into the black water. This act, if the telling is not too romanticized, must have been an awesome sight to Frobisher's men, whose spirits must have been lifted by the spectacle of their fearless captain.

The following morning, 14 July, the winds calmed, and the crew breathed a sigh of relief. They were adrift, but alive, perhaps the only human beings for leagues. The hull was dredged and the ship righted. The masts, fortunately including the main mast, which had survived, and the rigging were fixed as best they could. The aftermath of the storm had delivered them into a new world. On 22 July the west coast of Greenland was sighted, but again ice dissuaded the ship from heading inland, so the course was turned westward, land being sighted again on the 27th. This time it did not appear on any chart.

Frobisher at once determined to get ashore. In the twenty-first century, it is difficult to imagine the excitement of setting foot on a new land. Its literal equivalent would be a manned expedition to Mars. The giant opaque blue and white glaciers, never shrinking on the horizon, and tightly jostling ice packs prevented this for the time being, so the course went north, following the wall of ice on their portside, or larboard as it was to Elizabethan sailors. Added to the creaking of the ship's timbers would be the low booming of the breakers on the sides of the huge floes and the bumping of the broken shards of the ice packs tapping ominously on the ship's sides. At this point the ship was navigating its way up Baffin Bay, separating Labrador and Baffin Island from the west coast of Greenland, a completely new and alien environment. They were now further north than any Englishman had been before.

On the morning of 31 July a huge headland loomed on the horizon. So impressed by its sheer size, Frobisher was disposed to name this Elizabeth Foreland, but was still unable to explore further inland. The weather, now much improved, caused the ever technically minded Hall to take out the ship's longboat to a large glacier to take soundings of the depth of the ocean. A line and lead weight was all a man of Hall's expertise needed to calculate a depth of 16 fathoms, a more than navigable depth.

The following day a 'noyce as if a great cliffe had fallen into the sea' brought home the dangerous reality of the ice as the berg Hall had been standing on only a day earlier cracked apart and disappeared below the water, before slowly re-emerging at the surface and righting itself according to its new centre of gravity. Finally, on 10 August, after numerous sightings of land but frustrated efforts to get ashore, the winds and currents shifted causing the fortress of ice to yield and reveal the mouth of a bay, which to Frobisher was surely his passage to Cathay, when in reality it was a small inlet of Baffin Island. Once again, Hall, this time with a number of the crew, took out the longboat. This time they reached a small island, which is still known as Little Hall Island. Frobisher had promised Lok a token from the first successful landing. This 'token of Christian possession', as Best later dubbed it, became indicative of explorers 'laying claim' to newly discovered land. One of the crew, Robert Garrard, brought back a small, heavy black stone and gave it to Frobisher. This black rock was to secure the fortunes of the subsequent voyages, and conversely proved the ultimate undoing of many who had become involved.

The ice was now sufficiently clear for Frobisher to venture up the strait that had been revealed. To the south was the perceived north coast of America, to the north, Asia. In actual fact, they were sailing into an inlet of Baffin Island, the land to the south, Resolution Island, to the north, Lok's Land. The inlet itself became known as Frobisher Bay, a lasting memorial to the men who ventured there. The bay itself is riddled with a network of islands, perhaps 30 miles wide at its widest point and 185 miles long. The *Gabriel* was fortunate to arrive there in the season it did, as the bay is icebound for most of the year. Baffin Island is the largest in a group of islands to the north of Canada that make up the Arctic Archipelago. The island and the strait to the east of it were named after William Baffin, who took up the mantle of discovering the North-West Passage in the 1610s. Directly south of Baffin Island lies Labrador, the northernmost point of Newfoundland, and to the south-west, a much more significant body of water, Hudson Bay, stretches right down to Ontario.

Henry Hudson thoroughly explored this bay in 1610, and it became a hugely important and lucrative base for the expanding fur trade with the French and local Indians, as well as the burgeoning whaling fleets headed by the Hudson's Bay Company. It is perhaps ironic that, had ice floes not prevented Frobisher from turning west earlier, history may tell of the successful Frobisher Bay Company. He was only therefore, if the reader will excuse the pun, at the tip of the iceberg. But he was the first, a precursor for generations of Arctic explorers, who continued to open up the mysteries and potential of the Arctic regions of North America.

None of this would have concerned Frobisher, who believed he was now on the final stage of his journey to the marketplaces of the East. He named the waterway Frobisher Strait, as Magellan had done at the other end of the world. Having nearly reached the end of the bay, the increasing number of small islands made navigation more difficult, if not impossible and Hall and Frobisher went ashore to seek high ground and assess the situation. According to Lok, from this vantage point Frobisher 'Saw far the two hed lands at the . . . end of the straiets and no likelyhood of land to the northwards of them (nor) between them (which) they judged to be the West Sea, whereby to pas to Cathay and to East India.' Why did Frobisher and Hall believe they had found a clear passage through when 12 miles away the bay ended and gave way to hundreds of miles of solid land? The reasons for this are numerous. A simple matter of weather, cloud cover or low-lying fog would have made a distance of a few miles difficult to recognize fully, coupled with the low-lying topography of the land that stretched out beyond the bay. There are also the insufficiencies of knowledge pertaining to topography and the measurement of land height and distance. The appearance of small islets was not unheard of in navigable waters. Indeed,

Magellan had encountered similar difficulties travelling to South America, so perhaps it was the same situation here. Then there is the question of false belief. The voyage had thus far been disastrous. As far as Hall and Frobisher were concerned, the *Gabriel* was all that remained of the expedition, and they would perhaps have been reticent about accepting that the route was impassable after such hardships. Frobisher's temperament is worth considering here. He was a gambler by inclination; he gambled with his life at Mina, with prosecution and imprisonment as a privateer, his loyalties as a spy and he had most certainly gambled with the life of his crew. Even on his return Lok states: 'he vowched . . . absolutlye with vehement words, speeches and oaths, that he had . . . discoverid [an] open passage into the South Sea . . . which goethe to Cathai'.

From his vantage point, it was not only the landscape that Frobisher surveyed. He noticed a number of small boats rowing towards their position. The group of Inuit in their kayaks had doubtless seen the *Gabriel* enter the bay. Typically fearful and suspicious, Frobisher rushed to the boat and reached the *Gabriel* before he realized that the Inuit camp was at the base of the hill he had been standing on and that they were merely heading home. Fears slightly allayed, Frobisher, Hall and three crewmen cautiously went ashore to meet the natives. In a move more than familiar to Frobisher, Hall was exchanged for an Inuit man who was taken back to the *Gabriel*. Once aboard, the Inuit man was fed and watered, but did not appear fond of English food or wine. The reasons for this became clear on subsequent meetings when the Inuit brought their own food with them: '. . . salmon and raw flesh, which they would greedily devour to the great amazement of the men'.[2]

Once it was established that neither side wished the other real harm, trading began, and Inuit men, women and children came aboard the *Gabriel*: '. . . they exchanged coats of seal and bear skins . . . for belts, looking glasses and other toys'.[3] They were seemingly unfazed by the ship, probably due to its similarity to Norse vessels which had been using the waters for over 300 years. Indeed, men joined in competition with each other, climbing the rigging and performing acrobatics: 'To show their agility, they tried many stunts upon the ropes of the ship and seemed to have strong arms and nimble bodies'.[4]

Inuit culture and the impact of this first contact with the English will be fully considered in a later chapter, but there are significant elements that are worthy of note here. The Inuit would have been a marvel to the English; not only their customs, but their appearance. Likened to Tartars and Lapps encountered on other voyages, this would add great weight to Frobisher's claim to have arrived in or near China. With broad faces, flat noses and straight, dark hair, they fitted the ideal of an Asian people perfectly.

For once, Hall broke off from his staid technical log and made time to write on this part of the journey. He appears to have been a keen anthropologist, fascinated by buildings, customs and language. He attempted to write out some of the Inuit language phonetically:

Pollevetagay – Knife
Accarkay – Boat
Cangnawe – Nose[5]

In the 1930s, linguistics expert William Thalbitzer analyzed Hall's work from the first voyage and compared it with terms in Greenland Inuit dialect of the time. He makes the point that pronunciation, with elided vowels and inevitable slurrings, would have proved very difficult for Frobisher's men.

Whilst ashore, Hall made note of the stone buildings, which he saw as meeting houses, and smaller tents of sealskin. He also observed Inuit weaponry and fishing tools. This is in stark contrast to Frobisher via Best who was ever suspicious of the Inuit. On first encounter he said he was enticed towards an Inuit, only to find a number hiding behind a rocky outcrop, intent, he thought, on ambush. Perhaps Frobisher's overly cautious suspicion was well-founded, based on what happened next.

By 19 August the first Inuit to come aboard the *Gabriel* was in the employ of the English, or so they thought. A selection of gestures and broken phrases in different languages had led the misguided captain to believe he now had a guide to navigate them through the non-existent sea to the west. They sent him ashore with five crewmen to collect his kayak. Frobisher gave instructions to alight in clear sight of the *Gabriel*. Imagine his consternation then when the little boat rounded a headland and disappeared. Perhaps they had wished to conduct a little one-to-one trade; a fur pelt for a few buttons was a good deal. The guide and three crewmen went ashore, leaving two men in the boat, which could still be seen by Frobisher. But suddenly they began to row around the headland and also disappeared from view. Perhaps their companions were in trouble and needed their aid, or perhaps they had been cautious initially and, seeing their fellows welcomed into the Inuit settlement, decided to join them by the fireside with the promise of a warm tent and furs. Whatever their fate, the five men were never again seen by English eyes. The crew of the *Gabriel* assumed, not unreasonably, that they had been killed, and based on what they had seen of Inuit diet, potentially eaten.

This severely tarnished the future relationship between the two groups. Exchanges between the English and Inuit were very variable, tribal warfare was common and neighbours were rarely always friends. In 1583, John Davis established good relations with Inuit in Greenland, so much so that on his return in 1585 both groups recognized each other as friends.

Both trips, however, were peppered with skirmishes with the Inuit. During the second and third voyages, Frobisher had both peaceful and aggressive encounters with the natives. Though the five men were gone, they were not forgotten and their fate was pursued again during the second voyage. Neither, it appears were they forgotten by the Inuit. The Victorian journalist Charles Hall sheds light on another version of their story. Whilst searching for the definitive fate of the unfortunate Franklin party who had disappeared in 1845, he came across an oral tradition that was rich and varied, dating back generations. Amongst the tales he was told was one of five Kabloona, the accepted Inuit word for Europeans, who wintered with their ancestors and then built a boat and sailed away. Later in this book examination of Hall's interviews will pose many interesting questions and provide insight into Frobisher's impact on the Inuit landscape and people.

As the five men had rowed out in the only boat available, Frobisher was essentially helpless to go to their aid as he could not risk beaching the *Gabriel*. Instead he had to wait. The gunner fired the canonette, the trumpeter sounded a bugle call in an attempt to get a response from the sailors, but none came. Perhaps strangely, if they feared reprisals, the Inuit continued to float around the *Gabriel* in their kayaks. Recognizing the would-be guide, Frobisher enticed him towards the ship with the promise of a large bell. As he reached to take the trinket, Frobisher '. . . suddenly dropped the bell, grabbed the man and plucked him out of the sea . . .'.[6] He is said to have done this, kayak and all, which is perhaps more artistic licence than an accurate representation of his strength. Regardless, the English now had a bargaining chip. Surprisingly, no exchange was offered, and with no means of getting ashore and with increasingly heavy snow fall, they had no choice but to abandon the five to their fate and set the *Gabriel* on a course for home.

Returning home on 9 October 1576, they were proclaimed as heroes, delivered from the depths, and their captive proof of their travelling to a strange and distant land: 'This new prey was sufficient witness of Frobisher's distant voyage . . . for no one had ever before seen or heard of such a strange infidel.'[7] He was a spectacle, and although he did not survive the year, succumbing to an alien fever that his body could not take, he had served to send interest in further voyages into an upward spiral. Investors jostled for position, much to the delight of Michael Lok, despite the voyage actually returning £1,500 in the red.

The black rock that Frobisher had taken as first evidence of land sat in Lok's house. He had sent it to several assayers with no positive results. He pressed on, perhaps out of desperation to find some material gain beyond a dead Inuit to secure profits, and approached an Italian alchemist, Giovanni Agnello. Alchemy has an unsettled reputation. On the one hand, it was a philosophical quest to understand the complexities of the universe and perhaps to acquire immortality; to that end some alchemists sought the elusive elixir of life. On the other, it represented the beginnings of inorganic chemistry and practical science.

One area that was not practical was the search for the philosopher's stone, a method to turn base metal into gold. Frobisher's ore might well have been the key to the whole mystery, hence the enthusiasm of Lok and Agnello. Both men, of course, overlooked the basic economics of the matter. If the means to turn base metal into gold could be found, then gold would be as common (and relatively worthless) as iron. There could be no fortune in that.

Agnello's results were very different. He gave Lok a piece of gold that he had supposedly refined from the black rock. Lok acted quickly. He approached Walsingham with a letter for Elizabeth in addition to the piece of gold that Agnello had extracted. Lok could have saved himself the trouble of employing assayers, as Best writes: 'One of the pieces [of ore] was given to a gentlewoman, the wife of one of the adventurers . . . she threw it into the fire . . . when it was taken out . . . it glistened with a bright marquesset of gold'.[8]

Walsingham, however, remained dubious of Agnello's findings. Alchemy was a circumspect and secretive practice, associated with the black arts and even devil worship, and he insisted on having his own assayers take a look. They found no gold, but a small amount of silver and tin. This had given Lok's persuasive financial mind time to prepare some figures. With the help of Agnello, he hypothesized that a net profit of £20 could be extracted from each ton of ore in precious metals, which would seriously swell the national treasury with a suggested 300 tons of ore to be brought back, and a third promised to the Crown. Walsingham's assayers had not found gold, but they had found silver. Who knew what precious material this ore might yield?

The figures were too attractive to pass up and Walsingham agreed to grant a patent to Lok for a further voyage. Frobisher had been left out of the loop at this point, despite enquiring about the rock several times. Perhaps Lok was erring on the side of caution, but, once the ore had reached Walsingham, whispers began to run around court. Frobisher had become the figurehead, he was essential for the voyage to go ahead, particularly if this new sideline was to be kept between a select few. Many would invest based purely on the fact that Frobisher had led the last voyage; indeed, Lok had already decided to limit the number of investors, as there were so many, the potential for profit was negligible. It was time to change the focus. Frobisher was no longer looking for a passage to China and India, he now had a more pressing and profitable quarry. Gold.

Chapter 6

Golden Boy

Frobisher, no longer social pariah, pirate and thief, was now celebrated wherever he went. The 'riches' of the ore he had discovered were the subject of much gossip, despite it being a supposed state secret. The value of the ore had grown in the telling, from the voyager's wife throwing what she assumed was coal into the fire and it turning into burnished gold, to court poet Philip Stanley writing to his French friend Hubert Languet saying that the ore turned into pure gold. The assayers' valuations soared from £20 profit per ton to over £200. Elizabeth, normally tight with her purse strings, invested £1,000 in the venture, much to the chagrin of members of the Privy Council. They kept a close eye on Frobisher's expenditures, particularly with regard to man power, capping the crew at 120 men, although Frobisher squeezed a few extra gentleman–adventurers on board. Frobisher's petition to the Queen for the second voyage still exists. She also pledged a Royal Navy ship, the *Ayde*, as flagship for the voyage, a 200–tonner with a large hold to carry plenty of the precious black rock.

The ship cost £750, the barques *Gabriel* and *Michael* £400 each. The total to equip them with food, wages, guns and provisions came to a staggering £4,400, although this was negligible in terms of the expected returns of new territory paved with gold. The provisions for the three ships included 16 tons of biscuits, 30 tons of meal, 80 tuns of beer, 5 tuns of malmsey and sack (wine for the officers), 5 tons of beef, 15½ tons of pork, 10 tons of peas, 2½ tons of fish stock, butter, cheese, oatmeal, rice, honey, wood, sea coal, charcoal, fishing nets, almonds, liquorice, clothes (hats, jerkins, hose, doublets) and money for the surgeons to fill their chests.

Further to this, the Queen created a commission to oversee preparations. This included Michael Lok and William Wynter, Master of Ordnance for the Navy, doubtless to keep a mindful eye on her investment. However, Wynter was as gripped by gold-rush fever as anyone, having spoken to the alchemist Agnello and the assayer Jonas Schutz, who joined the second voyage.

By the sixteenth century, the early Christian belief that Eve had taken the philosopher's stone out of Eden seems to have disappeared, but by that time too the 'science' of alchemy had identified the stone's key component as an element called carmot. The eighth-century alchemist Jabir ibn Hayyan believed that since all elements had various properties, a re-arrangement of these properties could result in something else. The change would be affected by a dry red powder called al iksir (elixir) derived from the stone.

By the eleventh century philosophers like ibn Sina (Avicenna in the European translation) were casting doubts on all this, but in Europe itself Albertus Magnus claimed to have rediscovered the stone two centuries later. Theophrastus von Hohenheim, better known as Paracelsus, died when Frobisher was eight years old. A much-travelled doctor and alchemist, he promoted the idea of observation and deduction as systems of scientific enquiry but also believed in alkahest, of which the elements of earth, fire, water and air were derivative forms. To Paracelsus, alkahest *was* the philosopher's stone.

Jabir's theory, accepted by one of the highest authorities of the sixteenth century (Paracelsus himself), was that gold and silver could be hidden in alloys and ores, hence the excitement generated by Frobisher's black rock. At the end of March, William Wynter and others reported that Frobisher's claims for the North-West Passage were viable and effectively gave the go-ahead for the second voyage.

So, with a royal seal of approval and the potential of huge returns, investors began clamouring at the door of Michael Lok. Warwick and Burghley doubled their stake to £100 and Walsingham, who had seen the ore first hand, pledged £200. Perhaps unsurprisingly as a keen advocate of alchemy, John Dee ventured £25. Other new investors included the Countess of Warwick, Anne Russell, wife of Ambrose Dudley. She had become a fervent supporter of the cause, and her husband had successfully petitioned the Muscovy Company on behalf of Frobisher. She was also one of the Queen's closest female friends, famed for her academic brilliance and beautiful voice. She would sit by Elizabeth's bedside years later when the Queen was dying.

Even before the promise of gold was on the table, Anne had commissioned Richard Willes to write a tome on accounts of travels in Asia to help promote the voyages. As demonstrated by the quotation given at the beginning of Chapter 4, Willes was more of a realist than his contemporaries, carefully considering the pros and cons of trying to navigate a passage to the North-West, without the overblown posturing of Gilbert. Even so, the voyage took on a more grandiose air. Though no formal charter was created, Lok dubbed the commission the Cathay Company. With royal support and such a high profile, it was hardly necessary to ensure a monopoly on routes to the West, as no Englishman or trading company could compete with the level of investment in the project. Frobisher was given the title 'captain-general' and ultimate authority over the expedition; this was largely to nurse his ego. It had originally been intended for him to share the role with his second-in-command, Edward Fenton, but Frobisher had flown into a rage saying he would go alone or not all. It was in fact Fenton who calmed Frobisher, proving the committee had made the right choice in appointing him as a foil to Frobisher's temper, just as Hall and Griffyne had been on the previous voyage. Although it would appear at this point that he was a man of better temperament, Fenton's career mirrors that of Frobisher's to a certain extent. In 1582, he was sent, supported by Leicester, to round the Cape of Good Hope and approach the North-West Passage from the other side. This was a spectacular failure. Fenton, in constant deadlock with his officers, for he was as capable of flights of temper as Frobisher, got no further than Brazil, and, also like Frobisher, he abandoned hope of fame and fortune as an explorer. Later he would seek to distinguish himself against the Armada as commander of the *Mary Rose*.

With the *Ayde* as flagship, the resilient *Gabriel* and *Michael* completed the fleet. The crew, numbering 120, included miners and assayers to excavate and examine the ore. The crew also included a number of convicts, in keeping with Gilbert's suggestions. These were to be left in Friseland and the Frobisher Strait to winter there and explore the surrounding areas. This is the first attempt by England to settle a newly discovered land, something that was further promoted on the third voyage, and became a primary objective in all further English expansion and exploration. Something of the essence of this is captured by J.H. Elliott in *Europe Divided 1559–1598*: 'The very fact of America's existence, and of its gradual revelation as an entity in its own right, rather than as an extension of Asia, constituted a challenge to a whole body of traditional assumptions, beliefs and attitudes.'[1] In other words, Englishmen were now not merely looking for a way *through* these strange lands, but were interested in the lands themselves.

It appears that the convicts absconded before the expedition left port, perhaps after crossing the captain-general's palm with coin. Despite Frobisher's temper tantrums, the commission were determined that he should have his priorities mapped out for him, with such large amounts at stake. First and foremost, he was to return to Little Hall Island and its environs, and set about mining for as much ore as possible. If the assayers deemed it valuable, he should load the ships' holds leaving 'other superfluous things'. Then there was the search for the five lost sailors from the first voyage. At all times, the English were keen to gain a foothold in new lands, particularly to prevent their continental cousins from getting involved, and so, in addition to finding good harbours, Frobisher was to maintain good relations with the natives, something that was against type, as will be shown. Generally speaking, the whole history of European settlement in the New World was one of condescension that was based on bigotry. Europeans saw themselves as superior, not merely because their skin was white, but because they were Christian. Still later generations from Britain would come to believe that God was an Englishman.

The backers also wanted him to bring back one or two more examples of the native population as a double standard; the use of force was neither encouraged nor prohibited. Should there be no sign of ore, which all thought doubtful, he was to resume his search for Cathay, sending the *Ayde* back to protect the Queen's investment. If possible, crewmen should be left ashore to winter and explore the new-found lands. Frobisher had already requested additional wool and linen for clothing to protect the men from the colder climate he had experienced in summer at Baffin Island. No one could even guess at the harsh privations an Arctic winter would bring.

On 31 May (Whitsunday), the fleet left Blackwall in fair weather; aboard the *Ayde*, Frobisher and his pilot master Hall, for the *Gabriel*, Fenton, described by Settle as 'a gentleman of Lord Warwick's', and the *Michael*, Gilbert York. Dionysus Settle provides the most detailed account of the second voyage, and this is his only known work. Settle wrote it for the Earl of Cumberland, which was a common practice for any writer seeking a patron. Marlowe and Shakespeare did the same twenty years later. And Settle was particularly canny because Cumberland was also Lord of Skipton in Yorkshire, so he was able to claim Frobisher as a 'fellow countryman'.

The first port reached was Orkney, where, in high spirits, the crew caused locals to flee, believing them to be an invasion force. After being persuaded that the Englishmen wanted to trade, the Orcadians exchanged fresh fish and meat for clothes and shoes. Settle was amazed at the Orcadian's behaviour: 'It seemeth they are often frighted with Pirates . . . that moveth them to such sudden fear'.[2] He was also appalled at the poverty of the islanders, a quarter of a century before Scotland was foisted on the English by virtue of the Stuart succession. Their houses were hovels and domestic animals shared the accommodation with their masters. They used peat and cow-pats for fires, having so little wood, and ate meat without salt. Their money was 'base', their clothes 'the rudest sort' in Scotland. Settle gives the impression he was not sorry to leave.

Hall's log for this journey has unfortunately not survived, so it is not possible to pinpoint this expedition's locations with the same degree of certainty. Settle was a gentleman-venturer who had joined the expedition out of sheer curiosity. He was not a navigator, but his account must suffice. By 4 July, after nearly a month without sight of land, they came to the south coast of Greenland, or, as they knew it, Friseland. What astonished Settle most was the lack of darkness. 'We had no night', which gave him the opportunity to read at all hours. Still unable to negotiate the icy coastline inland, the course turned directly west. Settle saw huge floating logs he assumed to have been uprooted by floods inland and 'great islands of ice, of half a mile, some more, some less, in compass, showing above the sea 30 or 40 fathoms [180–240ft]'.[3]

The journey across Baffin Bay was stormy for a short time, but it was not enough to trouble the *Gabriel* or *Michael* and certainly not the giant flagship, which was far more suited to transatlantic crossings. Settle expected birdsong and the sweet scent of gum trees (he had obviously been reading too much Mandeville) and instead got 'the most boisterous Boreall blasts, mixed with snow and hail'.[4] On 17 July the fleet once again reached the mouth of Frobisher Bay, the Queen's Foreland. The captain-general boarded a pinnace with a number of assayers and miners on board to search Little Hall Island for the black rock; other pinnaces were sent out to the surrounding area with the same mission. Little Hall Island was aptly named at barely a mile square, so a search would not take long. A lump came in to Frobisher's throat, his heart pounded in his eardrums. Where was the ore? This had been the place where Robert Garrard had picked up the original stone that had served the expedition so well. Where was the rest? Fortunately, the reports from elsewhere were more fruitful. To a miner or assayer, a trace of iron oxide here, some shimmering mica or a vein of quartz there could signal the presence of precious metals. This was great news, the ships' cannon roared their approval down the bay in celebration and the following day, after a feast of seal and roast bird, they climbed a hill on Little Hall Island dubbed Mount Warwick, to stake their claim as the first Englishmen on North American soil. The cairn that was built to mark this occasion survives to this day. A rather meagre pile of stones that signifies the auspicious beginnings of an industrious, if fruitless mining centre, its significance in the landscape has shifted, as will be shown in a later chapter, having different cultural importance to the local inhabitants.

On returning to the boats, the English noticed that a group of Inuit had reached the top of Mount Warwick, and were calling out to the sailors. Settle takes up the tale: 'Some of the people of the country showed themselves, leaping and dancing with strange shrieks and cries.'[5] On hearing the trumpeter sound a peal in reply, they danced and seemed to be very pleased, as Best notes: 'they delighted in music of any kind'.[6] Despite their rather one-dimensional view, Best's writings and those of Settle are useful. It is through Best that we learn of the level of communication between the two groups, predominantly sign language, and through both, of their culture and attire. There is a tendency in these writings toward negativity and disgust. To Frobisher's men, these were 'savages' of a non-Christian culture. This time, unlike the previous voyage, trade was conducted in a far more suspicious manner, probably as native and explorer remembered the events of the previous year, with losses on both sides: 'the

natives seemed very anxious to confer with our people . . .
neither party trusted the other enough to visit them in their
own territory . . .'.[7] The fears were reasonable, as Frobisher and
Hall, mindful that returning with a native was one of their
priorities and in need of an interpreter, signalled for a number
of Inuit to come and meet them. Two obliged and the captain-
general and his pilot made the approach, but on trying to
capture them, the Inuit broke free and succeeded in laying
hand to their bows. Frobisher, whilst being chased down the
headland, received an arrow in the backside, a suitably ignoble
injury for trying to trap the two Inuit. Musket fire scattered the
natives into retreat and one Nicholas Conger 'being a
Cornishman, and a good wrestler' made chase and succeeded
in capturing one of the men. This would certainly not be the
last time that the English would have contact with this group
of Inuit, and they were to meet others along the way. They
probably assumed they were all from the same tribe, although
the contemporary accounts do not discuss this.

For the next two days the fleet was pinned down by a gale,
and with no encampment yet set up on land and no way of
safely getting there, the ships offered most shelter. Settle says
that the crew were kept on watch constantly in case the ice
closed in around them. When the winds abated, the three ships
entered the bay. Ship's mate aboard the *Michael*, Charles
Jackman, identified a suitable anchorage on the tip of the
southern coast of the bay, duly named Jackman Sound. Here
they found the body of an extraordinary creature, like a fish,
but with a long helical tusk. Settle wrote: 'On this West shore
we found a dead fishe floating which had in his nose a horn
straight and torque (spiralled) of length two yards lacking two
inches.'[8] The tip was broken and some of the sailors put
spiders into the cavity in the belief that spiders were attracted
to gold. In fact, the creatures died. 'We supposed it to be a Sea
Unicorne'.[9]

This was the subject of many a unicorn legend, the narwhal.
Indigenous tales vary slightly but one common theme is of a

woman or girl falling into the sea where her hair was twisted into a spiral by the waves to form a tusk, the girl herself turning into a narwhal. From the literal Inuit translation, 'He Who Can Easily Curve Himself Against The Sky', in the wild the male narwhal tusks do thrust toward the heavens as they swim through the icy waters of Greenland and the Canadian Arctic, which are their home. The ivory itself was thought to have magical properties and to be an antidote to any poison; it was worth more than its weight in gold. It is still highly prized, fetching thousands of pounds for a whole tusk, but its sale and harvest are now heavily regulated. The Inuit, as many subsistence cultures do, used the whole animal for food, oil and functional and ritual objects, such as hairpins, sled skis and amulets.

As English influences spread, the Inuit began to hunt narwhal purely for their tusks as they started to settle into European-style villages and townships. The myth surrounding the narwhal had already been dispelled by a contemporary source, but Frobisher's men would have been unaware of this as it was not translated into English until over a century later.

Olaus Magnus was a Swedish ecclesiast and writer living in Rome under the auspices of the Pope. He was also a keen historian and geographer and in 1539 produced his exquisite *Carta Marina*, the most accurate map of mainland Europe at the time, although it was never put into general circulation and became lost until the mid-nineteenth century. To accompany this, he produced a pictorial history and natural history 'Historia de gentibus septentrianalibus'. He drew on tales of fishermen and his knowledge of Scandinavian legend, as well as his considerable skill as a draughtsman. Despite the book being filled with fantastical beasts and tales, such as dwarves fighting giant crane in his native Sweden, Magnus does correctly identify some animals, including the walrus and 'narwal', although he erroneously placed its horn on top of its head in his description. The tusk was the first prize to go into the hold of the *Ayde*. It was presented to Queen Elizabeth as a gift on Frobisher's return. Most sources say she used it as a sceptre, and it was set with jewels and gold, at a cost akin to that of building a new castle. This would seem plausible as narwhal ivory has such an exalted history, but others suggest it was used at parties by the Queen, an amusement for making phallic jokes, something of which the playful Queen was not entirely incapable.

But back on the second voyage there was still ore to be found. The fleet had been in the bay for close to a month and yet their hulls were devoid of any of the black rock. The *Michael* and *Gabriel* sailed from the south to north coast of the bay, close to where the previous landing parties had found evidence of the ore. One island lay just around the headland from Little Hall Island. It was sheltered from the tides (although not the increasingly biting wind), and had good views to the north to Baffin Island and to the south into the waters of the bay. It was covered with outcrops of the black rock, and therefore Frobisher determined this should be their base camp. It was dubbed Countess of Warwick Island, known today as Kodlunarn Island. All that remains of the mines that were opened there are two trenches, deep gashes in the cliffs.

Mining was not a science of controlled explosions, diggers and drills. In England, the little coal mining that went on was open-cast, merely hacking away on the surface. The ground on Kodlunarn would have been cleared by pickaxe and mattock, and then steel wedges would have been hit with lump hammers to split apart the rock. It was back-breaking labour, and several of the miners ended up lame or with ruptured spleens due to the huge amounts of physical exertion involved.

The archaeological survey of the island, conducted by William Fitzhugh and Susan Rowley in the 1980s, provides great insight into the formation of the camp. A rectilinear foundation, containing blackened earth, slag and charcoal, evidence of burning, has been identified as a smithy. There were two blacksmiths on the second voyage and they would have been engaged in the repair and sharpening of mining

An inaccurate early map of the Arctic.

An imaginative illustration of a kayak based on information derived from Frobisher's 1577 voyage to the Arctic.

A sixteenth-century astrolabe, one of the oldest navigational instruments available. This is a German variant, but because it was originally an Arab invention, it still retains Arabic designs on its brass face.

The cross staff in use by a sixteenth-century navigator, from a contemporary engraving.

A sundial and compass dating from the late sixteenth century. This one is probably unique because it also doubled as a powder flask for a firearm.

Highly polished ivory seal-head-shaped nozzle for a sealskin float, similar to the one offered to Frobisher on his second voyage. *(From the Bering Strait region, drawing by author from an example collected by Pitt Rivers, 1884)*

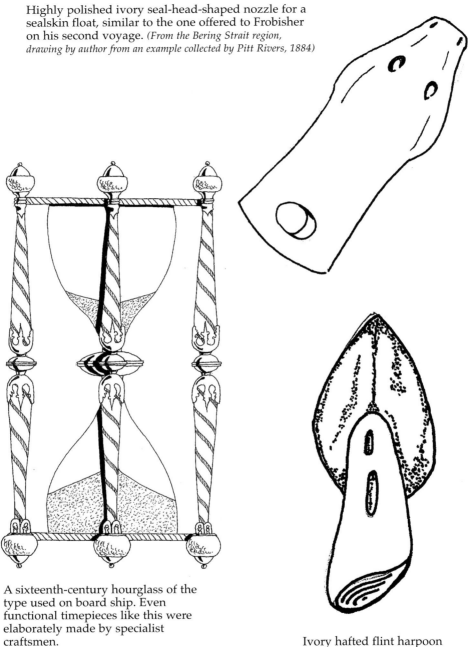

A sixteenth-century hourglass of the type used on board ship. Even functional timepieces like this were elaborately made by specialist craftsmen.

Ivory hafted flint harpoon head. The Inuit worked in both metal and stone. *(Drawing by the author from an example collected by Pitt Rivers, 1884)*

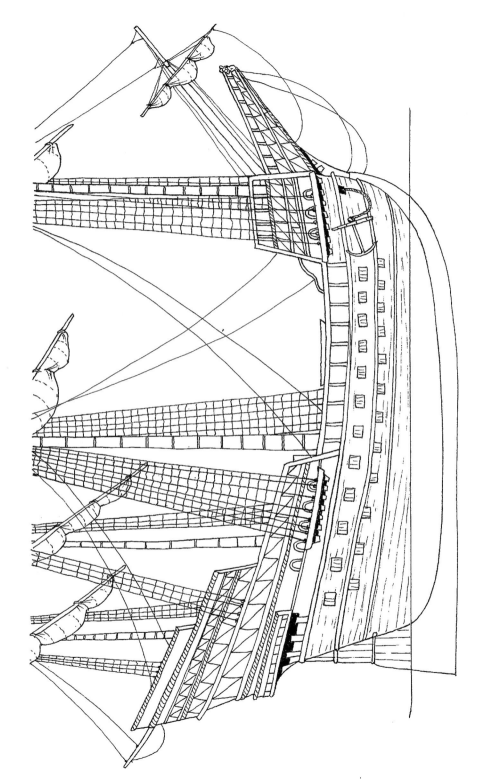

A diagrammatic representation of the 741-ton *Triumph*. As Frobisher's flagship in the Armada, it was the largest ship in either fleet and carried forty-six guns.

The Lower Pool looking across to Southwark. In Frobisher's day ocean-going ships sailed from the shore on the left of this photograph. *(Picture credit: Eloise Campbell)*

A sixteenth-century long house of the type built by Wynter on Kodlunarn Island. This is the English variant with the living quarters to the left and animal accommodation to the right. Because there were no trees available and much of the timber had been lost in storms, Wynter's carpenters would have had to improvise using stone and driftwood.

The Alchemist by Cornelis Pietersz Begijn, painted in 1663. By the time of this painting, pure chemistry was emerging from the mumbo-jumbo of alchemy. A century earlier, it was a common belief that Frobisher's ore contained a high quantity of gold which would have made him and England fabulously rich. Assayers like Jonas Schutz would have worked in chaotic conditions like this.

The generic memorial to Arctic explorers in King Edward VII Memorial Park, Shadwell. Ratcliff was the Quay from which Frobisher set sail for Meta Incognita. (*Picture credit: Eloise Campbell*)

THIS TABLET IS IN MEMORY OF
SIR HUGH WILLOUGHBY, STEPHEN BOROUGH,
WILLIAM BOROUGH, SIR MARTIN FROBISHER
AND OTHER NAVIGATORS WHO, IN THE LATTER
HALF OF THE SIXTEENTH CENTURY, SET SAIL
FROM THIS REACH OF THE RIVER THAMES NEAR
RATCLIFF CROSS
TO EXPLORE THE NORTHERN SEAS.

ERECTED BY THE LONDON. COUNTY COUNCIL 1922

A piece of ore taken from Meta Incognita. The double purpose of Frobisher's voyages was to explore and to bring back valuables. The ore proved to be iron pyrites – Fool's Gold.

A variant of the pistol carried by Frobisher in the painting by Cornelius Ketel. This particular version is an over and under double wheel-lock.

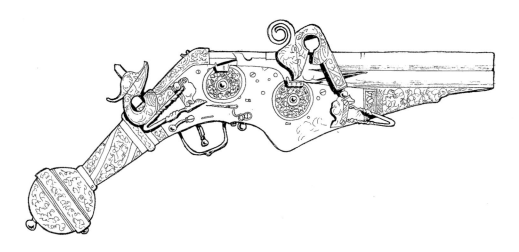

equipment. Ceramic crucible sherds were also found on this site. In the assaying process, the crucibles held molten ore and lead which was to alloy to the precious metals. The crucible would then be smashed leaving behind a lump of lead-coloured metal, not unlike the blooms found elsewhere on the site, but of a smaller size. These would then be reheated whereby the lead would melt away, leaving behind any precious metal. Other areas of burning, including a hearth and blooms, smooth metal formations, a by-product of metal work, suggest that the ore was being smelted on site to see what precious metals it might render.

The blooms, one of which was presented to the Smithsonian Institute by Charles Hall in 1864, cast an element of doubt on the chronology of the site. Recent carbon dating shows them to be at least a hundred years older than the dates of Frobisher's visits, giving them potential Norse origins. In an article written for the *Canadian Mineralogist* in 1986, Donald Hogarth and John Loop of the University of Ottowa had no doubts that the first mines were Frobisher's. The first excavation was from the Ship's Trench near tidewater, completed in 1577, and another in the centre of Kodlunarn known as Reservoir Trench in 1578. As one of the assayers wrote of the latter: 'The Countesse of Warwick myne fayled being so hard stone to breke.'[10] Whatever Hogarth and Loop's beliefs, the Inuit are also known to have made use of such blooms, from meteorites as well as man-made by-products. Frobisher had identified Kodlunarn as a suitable place to set up a base camp; perhaps the same was true of his Norse precursors. Another foundation containing broken tile and brick was the camp headquarters constructed during the third voyage, and became Fenton's House as time and material constraints had prevented the masons and carpenters from building a whole settlement. This was all that could be achieved and was the first house to be built by the English in the New World. These two structures were formed partially of stone, but charcoal deposits suggest that wood was available, despite there being no timber in the surrounding landscape. The third voyage, which consisted of a much larger fleet, was ravaged by storms, and some of the smaller boats were deemed irreparable. One of these, the *Dennis*, was sunk, so perhaps the wreckage had been put to good use. In the 1860s Hall makes mention of an abundance of driftwood, so perhaps the tide brought fuel and building material for the English. A timber longhouse would most likely have been shelter for the miners who laboured night and day, filling baskets with the precious black rock. This would not have sufficed as a winter dwelling as a timber building would not have provided enough insulation. They may as well have created a huge bonfire, even in August when the mining was in full swing because it was already bitterly cold. The final structure, to the north of the island, was a large stone, timber-framed building. This was the fortification and lookout post built by the fleet's lieutenant, George Best, known as 'Best's Bulwark'. As things were turning out, defence could be just what the English needed.

Whilst the mine was being established on Kodlunarn, the three vessels continued to travel along the coastal waters of the bay exploring inlets and islands. They had found more rock, in addition to a stone tomb containing a skeleton. The English assumed that the non–Christian savages who lived on these islands could not have cared for their dead in such a way. The fact that the body had been reduced to a bleached white skeleton also added to the miscomprehension that they were dealing with cannibals. They questioned their captive, whom they called Kalicho, on this, but again, due to lack of communication, the English readily stuck to their own conclusions. They continually quizzed him over the fate of the five sailors lost in 1576. Although communication was basic and limited, Kalicho vehemently denied their having been cannibalized after the English made gestures to mimic eating. The *Ayde* came upon an abandoned Inuit camp where they found a shirt, doublet and shoes. Surely these belonged to their hapless comrades and perhaps they were still alive? A few items of discarded clothing could well have been collected by the Inuit; it is known they made use of building materials from the abandoned camp at Kodlunarn and used the cairn on Mount Warwick as a centre for ritual and tradition. The sailors themselves could have discarded these clothes in favour of furs and skins. Perhaps they had traded them with the Inuit, or become assimilated into their culture, though judging from the reactions of their fellow mariners, this is unlikely. No, there was one option and one option only; these non-Christian savages, devoid of the emotions of humanity, either still had the five as captives or had killed and eaten them.

The *Ayde* put into the adjacent bay and sent men over the headland to surprise the Inuit encampment. By the time they got there, the tents had been struck and the camp was gone. This is not surprising; the Inuit, a non-sedentary, semi-nomadic people would have set up temporary seasonal camps wherever the fishing was best or caribou most plentiful. The English headed further up the bay until they reached another camp of about twenty Inuit and where they launched an attack. Startled, the Inuit took to their kayaks. Frobisher's men fired a volley to signal the *Ayde*, lying in wait around the headland. The Inuit were forced aground where they made a stand to defend themselves. Their chances were slim at best. They were facing muskets and crossbows, and the range of their weaponry, bows and darts, was insufficient. As part of the ritual and magic of the hunt, a hunter was to get as close to his kill as possible; the bow as a long-range weapon was an alien concept to them. About five or six Inuit were killed in the skirmish, the site of which became known as 'Bloody Point'. Best recalls: 'when they found they were mortally wounded, being ignorant what mercy meaneth . . . they cast themselves into the sea . . . for they supposed use to be like canibales'.[11] Best's usual blinkered view draws the wrong conclusion, but probably suggests an accurate motive for the Inuit suicides. Settle assumes the same bias, complaining that if only the natives had not committed suicide, they would have saved them and also treated their wounds: 'But they, altogether voyde of humanitie and ignorant what mercy meaneth, in extremities look for no other than death.'[12]

The skirmish took place on the south bank of the bay, where there had been no previous contact with the indigenous population. It might have been that the armed men who charged up the bay were the first white Europeans these Inuit had seen, and it was hardly a friendly introduction; men in iron breastplates and morions, using the fire-sticks that brought death at long range. The English who were ashore pushed inland to try to find those who had fled. Amongst the rocks they found an old woman, whose wrinkled face and appearance made them believe her to be a witch. Settle wrote: 'The old wretch, whom divers [some] of our sailors supposed to be either a devil or a witche, plucked off her buskins [boots] to see if she were cloven-footed and for her ugly huwe [colour] and deformitie, we let her go.'[13] Witchcraft in England was a common felony, which was punished by hanging. Periodically, there were outbreaks of witch fever at home, most recently in the 1560s. Faced with the unknown of an alien culture, Frobisher's men would have been prepared for the worst. They also found a young woman with an injured child. Leaving the old woman, they took the mother and child aboard the *Ayde*. They named her Arnaq, simply 'woman', and the infant 'Nuturaq', 'child'. Aboard the *Ayde* the ship's surgeon dressed the baby's wound, but the mother quickly removed the poultice and licked the wound clean, fearful of this unknown medicine. No doubt this added to the English belief in the Inuits' savagery. By modern standards, of course, the abilities of the ship's surgeon would seem equally barbaric. In fact, human saliva is sterile under normal conditions and contains enzymes that are capable of cleaning the skin, and so her actions probably helped the healing process.

The *Ayde* returned to Kodlunarn with tales of the battle and with their new hostages. Settle described the encampments he saw: 'Their riches are neither gold, silver or precious

Draperie, but their said tents and boats, made of the skinnes of red Deare and Seale skinnes.'[14] To Settle, the Inuit dogs resembled wolves, then still found in the more remote parts of Britain. Fearing reprisals from the natives, the forty-strong military contingent aboard the fleet were brought ashore and 'Best's Bulwark' was built.

It would appear that this was done just in time as, a few days later, an Inuit camp appeared on the mainland to the north of Kodlunarn. They began to call and signal to the English across the water. This time Frobisher made use of his captives quickly, sending Arnaq onto high ground so she could be in plain view. It is uncertain whether she would have been known to these Inuit, neighbouring groups would rarely have come into contact with each other, and Arnaq had been taken some 124 miles away. It is more likely that they were looking for Kalicho, so Frobisher boarded a rowing boat with him and they crossed the short stretch of water to the camp. On arrival, it was clear that these were Kalicho's people. His emotional reunion prompted Best to make his first, and virtually only admission of humanity amongst the Inuit: 'They are very kind to one another, and greatly sorrowful for their friends'.[15] Settle's understanding of the sign language of the Inuit was that they had a king called Cacough, who was 'carried on men's shoulders and a man farre surmounting any of our company in bigness and stature'.[16]

What follows is a mixture of misunderstanding and mistrust. Kalicho talked at length, about what we shall never know. All the while Frobisher was frantically trying to communicate that he wished to have news of the five lost sailors, and was pleased when the Inuit approached him making signs of writing. Best makes note of the Inuit ability to mimic the English and also their use of sign language. It is difficult to assess how much information was exchanged between the two groups, or whether the Inuit believed that signing served to placate their visitors. The following day, a second meeting took place. Frobisher had written a letter intended for the five. It read:

> In the name of God, in whom weal believe, who I trust hath preserved your bodyes and soules amongst these Infidels, I commend me unto you. I will be glad to seeke by all meanes you can devise, for your deliverance, eyther with force, or with any commodities within my Shippes, whiche I will not spare for your sakes, or anything else I can doe for you. I have aboord, of theirs, a Man, a Woman, and a Childe, which I am contented to deliver for you, but the man which I carried away from hence last yeare, is dead in England. Moreover, you may declare unto them, that if they deliver you not, I wyll not leave a manne alive in their Countrye, And thus, if one of you can come to speake with me, they shall have the Man, Woman, or Childe in pawne for you. And thus unto God, whom I trust you do serve, in haste I leave you, and to him we will dayly pray for you, This Tuesdaye morning the seaventh of August, Anno 1577

> Yours to the uttermost of my power

> Martin Frobisher

> I have sent by these bearers, Penne, Inke, and Paper, to write backe unto me agayne, if personally you can not come to certify me of your estate.

The exchange done, the Inuit pointed to the sun and put up three fingers as if to signify there would be an answer in three days. The Inuit would not have understood the letter, with no written language of their own until 200 years later. This is perhaps just as well, for its threatening tone towards them would not have been well received. Perhaps in their discussions, Kalicho had spoken to them of the perceived importance of sign language. They may have already experienced this through communication with fishermen, or the Norse, who may have been the earlier traders Settle refers to concerning the Inuit custom of leaving goods for barter on the beach, rather than trading directly. Kalicho would have doubtless been surrounded by the expedition's many diarists and may therefore have understood the importance of writing. Then we must also consider the fate of his countryman. Whilst on board ship, Kalicho had been shown a painting of the Inuit who had died in England the year before. Although the Inuit were found to be creative two-dimensional draughtsmen (their ivory and bone carvings are exquisite), it is difficult to see what Kalicho would have made of this artwork. He is said to have openly wept in front of the painting and spoken to it. Did he perhaps think his old friend had been trapped in the painting? Did he see this as a memorial and therefore guess at what would be his own fate? This is another interpretation of the Inuit mimicry of writing, perhaps referring to the two-dimensional representation of their countryman.

For the next few days cautious trade was conducted by both sides: 'taking the things they mean to trade, they place them on the ground. Then they back away [waiting until the crew] place their merchandise on the ground and back away . . . then if they like what is being offered come forward and take it.'[17] On 11 August, the day of the supposed exchange, Frobisher was encouraged to come and meet with the Inuit, who carried an inflated bladder, possibly a waterskin or float, to barter for a spy glass. As he approached the small group of Inuit, he noticed that there were several more concealed behind the rocks. Sensing an ambush, the captain-general returned to the safety of Kodlunarn. A few days later an 'injured' Inuit was carried and left on the beach crying for help. A well-placed musket shot above his head miraculously cured him of his lameness and he fled. It was now clear to the English that no exchange was likely to take place, even if the five were still alive. By now, Settle is referring to the Inuit as 'craftie villains'. Before leaving the area, he wrote a description of the natives he had encountered:

> They are men of a large corporature and good
> proportion, their colour is not much unlike the Sunne
> burnte country man who laboureth daily in the sun for
> his living. They wear their hair something long and cut
> before, either with a stone or knife, very disorderly. Their
> women wear their hair long and knit up with two loops,
> showing forth on either side of their faces.[18]

He also noted the 'darke azure' of the tattooed decoration on
the women's faces and wrists.

The Inuit, Settle observed, ate their meat raw and drank ice
for water as the English sucked sugar candy at home. He was
horrified to find no sign of tables, stools or napkins, but
watched as the Inuit, up to their knuckles in blood, 'use their
tongues as apt instruments to licke [the bones] clean'. He was
fascinated by the use of dogs as beasts of burden – 'as we do
oxen and horses, to a sled or traile'. Some of this information
at least came from Kalicho – 'as the captive, whom we have,
made perfect signes'. The Inuit costumes made from skins,
sewn together with sinews, with the fur inside were often worn
three deep. They were held in place with bones.

It is obvious from Settle's writing that he, at least, realized
that the Inuit tents could not serve them all year round. The
party found abandoned houses made of stone and whalebone
with entranceways like oven doors. He was clearly describing
some sort of permanent igloo. As a gentleman-venturer, Settle
was naturally interested in Inuit weapons. Their bows were a
yard long (the equivalent of the medieval short bow in European
terms) and the strings sinews. The arrows had three types of
head, made of bone, stone and iron. To Settle, the Inuits' most
dangerous weapon was a sharpened bone, used like a rapier.

With the patronizing observation that is frequently found
among early European explorers' memoirs, Settle noted the
Inuits' love of 'anything that is bright or giveth a sound'. He
was unable to make much headway with their religion: 'What
knowledge they have of God or what idol they adore, we have
no perfect intelligence.'[19] In keeping with most travellers, he

believed the Inuit to be anthropophagic (cannibals). He based this on the starving Inuits' propensity to eat any flesh, hunted or found as carrion – 'smell it never so filthily'. It was, he wrote, 'a loathsome spectacle, either to the beholders or hearers'.[20]

Settle was plagued by 'gnattes', the bites of which easily caused infection, and came out with a classic non sequitur when he noted large herds of deer (actually caribou) but hardly any grass. In fact, caribou can subsist on very little, scraping the lichens and mosses from the permafrosted ground. The biting flies that annoyed Settle follow the caribou, often causing them to stampede to higher ground – a single animal can lose a pint of blood to these pests in a day, when the swarms are at their height. He was right, however, in his belief that conventional European agriculture would not work here.

As far as the topography of the area was concerned, Settle read the frequent ice falls to be evidence of earthquakes or thunder. He saw no rivers or streams and concluded there were none, unless they were buried deep underground by the ice. It shows his naivety that he supposed the ground was warm enough for running water below the ice-bound surface.

By the end of the month, it was clear the expedition should head homewards. The miners, their clothes and shoes tattered, were exhausted and disabled by their laborious work collecting nearly 200 tons of ore. The approach of winter was causing both the sea and the ships to ice over. The last night on Kodlunarn was marked with a bonfire, a volley of gunfire and perhaps somewhat subdued celebrations. The ships, laden with their precious cargo, set sail on 23 August.

The return journey was beset by bad weather, the fleet was separated and none of the ships escaped unscathed. The *Gabriel* lost its master, William Smith, and its boatswain to the mercy of the deep. The *Ayde*'s rudder was all but destroyed, requiring a perilous repair at sea, and the *Michael*'s main mast snapped. Despite these problems, by 23 September, all three ships were safely back in English waters. The *Ayde*, the last to arrive, met the *Gabriel* in port in Bristol, whilst the *Michael*, using the same route it had the previous year, had landed in Orkney and gone on to Great Yarmouth. Although the voyage had taken its toll on the bodies and spirits of the men, they once again returned triumphant. Settle records the loss of two men: 'one in the waye of God's visitation and the other homeward caste overboard with a surge of the sea'.[21] Triumphant Frobisher may have been, but this time, the voices of dissention began to mutter.

Chapter 7

Fool's Gold

By the time Frobisher appeared before Queen Elizabeth again he had clearly become a royal favourite, and this went to his head. A report on all three voyages compiled for the State Papers highlights this: 'Hereupon, Frobisher grew into such a monstrous mind, that a whole kingdom could not contain it, but already, by discovery of a new world, he was become another Columbus.'[1] Before he left on his third voyage, the Queen gave him a generous gift of a large gold chain. He had presented her with the famed narwhal tusk, a rich prize and something that was irksome to the financially minded Lok. Frobisher was once again the focus of attention at court and delighted people with tales of his exploits, which doubtless swelled his ego further. He was a celebrity, finally gaining the admiration and recognition he had been craving.

The three captives brought back were once again a fascination. They remained in Bristol – already assuming a new importance because of its position in the west in the context of the New World – but did not survive long enough to be presented to the Queen, something that disappointed the doctor who examined them more than their actual deaths. Dr Edward Donninge's two-page report, written in Latin as was still usually the practice amongst medical men, still survives. According to Best: 'when he founde himself in captivitie, for very choller and disdain, he bit his tong in twayne within his mouth'.[2]

Whilst in Bristol, the Inuit were observed by the public as an entertainment. Seyer's *Annals of Bristol*, compiled from earlier documents in the 1790s, reported Frobisher's return to Kingrode (the entrance to Bristol Harbour) 'from Cattai'. He brought ore: 'esteemed to be very ritch and full of gowlde. It was heavy and so hard that it would strike fire like flint.'[3] Of more immediate interest were Frobisher's captives: 'Callicho and a woman called Ignorth [*sic*]. They were savage people and fed only upon raw flesh.'[4]

Kalicho took to the Avon in his 14ft kayak and began hunting mallard as he would have hunted seabirds in his Arctic home – 'he would hit a ducke a good distance and not misse'.[5] The women of England, who had perhaps applied a little lead-based make-up in the fashion of their white-faced monarch, were fascinated by the blue-delineated tattoos on Arnaq's face. The water-colourist John White, who was to join Ralegh on his voyages to North America where he would sketch Indians, flora and fauna, found in the Inuit captives his new fascination. The images, clearly the most famous, are very detailed, down to the seams on Kalicho's hide jacket. He also depicted the decisive 'battle' at Bloody Point from hearing the tales of the returning adventurers. As with the previous captive, the three Inuit did not survive more than a few months. Kalicho, it is presumed, died from a collapsed lung, having developed breathing problems earlier as a result of sustaining two broken ribs perhaps during his capture by Nicholas Conger. This death comes rather longer after the injury than is normal for pneumothorax and is more probably to be attributed to tuberculosis or even a simple cold. The woman died shortly afterwards from unknown causes. With only one native left, the baby was rushed from Bristol to London in the care of a nursemaid, but he too died before reaching the Queen. If unweaned, the child could well have died from an overwhelming immunological problem when faced with proteins in his diet with which he was entirely unfamiliar.

The meagre exploration of the new land gave rise to an increased desire to make it England's new territory. The Queen dubbed it Meta Incognita, meaning unknown limit, and the case for settlement was more aggressively followed on the third and final voyage. The academic John Dee drafted a map of this imagined new land, coining the phrase British Empire and went to great lengths to propose how such a mighty empire could be achieved, suggesting that a significant proportion of the Navy's budget should go towards such exploration, making it a royal priority rather than one left to private investors. In addition, as was the recourse for many academics at the time, he tried to tie in historical English claims to the territory.

Using the twelfth-century Welsh prince Madoc, who was alleged to have sailed west and made contact with the Indians known as the Mandan, he proposed that a North American colony had been set up and that the people living there were kinsmen to the English. He was unsuccessful in petitioning Elizabeth in the matter as he had taken into account cost and time factors, neither of which appealed to the frugal and impatient Queen. It was recognized by other investors that the idea of settlement was a sound one especially when looking at Spain's increasing wealth in Central and South America. The conquistadors had been successfully supplanting (and totally destroying) the Aztecs in Central America since the fifteenth century. The vast empire that had developed there included bases for sugar production and the slave trade with the majority of Spain's gold and silver coming from the mines of Mexico. The English eyed their new northern territory with the same degree of greed and avarice.

Dionysus Settle's account of the voyage was an instant bestseller of the day. Published in December 1577 it was translated into French, German and Latin. This spread the word of England's new venture and ears on the continent pricked up. The French ambassador in London wrote to Henri III saying that France could easily send its own expeditions. In fact, Frobisher told the Queen that Henry was arming twelve ships for just such a venture. From Moscow, Ivan the Terrible wrote of his concerns on hearing descriptions of the natives that the English were encroaching on his largely unknown domains in Siberia.

The Spanish ambassador, Bernardino de Mendoza, was far more interested and calculated. He had already planted a spy amongst the crew of the second expedition and was sending coded messages to Spain along with samples of the ore. Although the Spanish assayers correctly identified it as worthless, Spain still wanted to maintain their monopoly on colonization of the New World. It is not known who the agent or agents were. Mendoza's information is by turns accurate and misinformed. This could be due to the position his spy held. In the late 1990s, Donald Hogarth and Bernard Allarie found evidence to support a chief assayer, Robert Denham, as prime suspect. He would have known of the ore and its potential value, but not necessarily of the three natives who defeated thirty Englishmen, which Mendoza incorrectly reported. There was also a case for a double agent. Although the bearing of the location Mendoza reported is correct, the description of the bellicose nature of the Inuit could have been intended to dissuade him.

A possible other suspect could have been Edward Fenton. He was high in the chain of command, too high to be reproached by others. He lacked the respect of the men and had reason to resent Frobisher, with whom he was meant to have taken joint charge of the expedition. He would have been aware of the ships' positions and doubtless knew the inmost machinations of the Cathay Company, as he had been their chosen man. In support of this claim, Mendoza's report on planned attacks in the West Indies and the English intentions around the Cape of Good Hope in the 1580s makes no mention of Fenton, but lists all other officers involved by name. Further to this, his role in the English mission to India in 1582 was unsuccessful, perhaps deliberately so. As part of the Frobisher voyages, he was doubtless under the scrutiny of Walsingham, who was part of the project. How then did Mendoza gain any information of the delicacy he did? This gives credence to the possibility that Fenton was acting as a double agent. It is likely that he was working for pay, rather than simply being a Spanish sympathizer as he was commander of the *Mary Rose* against the Armada and therefore at that point at least loyal to the Crown of England. Mendoza's suspicions were very much confirmed when the cargo from the *Ayde* and *Gabriel* were placed under lock and key in Bristol's castle and the *Michael*'s cargo in the Tower. The English had something worth protecting, and worth hiding.

Assayers from all around the country and several from the continent set to work analyzing the tons of ore that had been brought back. The scientists with their varying methods were constantly battling to prove who was most accurate. Letters that have survived from November 1577 give us the flavour of the time, with impatience and petty rivalries being paramount: 'The three workmen [assayers],' wrote Michael Lok to Walsingham, 'are jealous of each other and loth to show their coining. The ore is very rich and will yield better than £40 a ton clear of charges. This is assuredly true . . .'.[6] Yet only two days later, William Wynter was expressing doubts: 'Albeit the ore does not appear to be of the value looked for.'[7]

And there were delays. From Bristol, Edward Fenton wrote to Walsingham that the ore was stashed safely in the castle, but work on the ships was overdue and the crew had not yet been disbanded or paid. Fenton particularly commended Henry Carew and hoped that all concerned would soon obtain 'Her Majesty's favour and recompense'.

At the end of November, Jonas Schutz fell ill and was unable to carry out his work on the ore. Others leapt into the breach. The assayer who produced the best results would get more pay and recognition and also perhaps become the chief assayer for future shipments. These conflicts are somewhat by the by as the results coming in told a different story from before. Agnello, the Venetian living in London who first reported on the ore's worth, found the refining of this ore 'succeeded not well'. Jonas Schutz, master assayer of the voyage, ultimately concluded after months at his furnaces that the ore was only worth £20 of gold, rather than the £240 he himself had calculated before the voyage. Frobisher, now ostensibly a rich man, employed Dr Burchard Kranich to carry out assays, building a furnace at his London home. Kranich, keen to gain the patronage and financial support of Frobisher, came up with altogether more promising results. However, where the full process had been observed for several of Schutz's assays, Kranich was only willing to let the committee watch the final stage of his, which brought the credibility of his results into question. Consequently, he was accused by many of adding silver and gold to the process. Kranich was not on top of his game either. In a letter to Walsingham at the end of November, he offered his services to the Queen as 'an expert and skilful man in minerals', but admitted his health was poor and he might not be able to deliver.

By the end of February 1578, Kranich was defending himself against charges of corruption in a letter to Walsingham – 'The exclamation to his honesty is without cause'[8] – and was reaffirming that he was better than Schutz in the assaying trade.

Michael Lok remained surprisingly optimistic. The first and second voyages had mounting debts but he had no compunction in approaching the Privy Council, who allowed him to add a 20 per cent surcharge onto investors' stakes. The investors agreed, equally buoyed by the public face of the voyage's success and largely unaware of the conflicting results of the assays. This at least paid the wages of Frobisher's men, who had been unable to leave the ships in port for two months; but Lok needed more. He wanted to build a mill, an industrial centre to refine the ore on a larger scale and therefore to increase profitability. He called this his 'great works' and set about finding a suitable site.

In January 1578, he settled on an area of the Darrent River near Dartford. Speed was of the essence and he employed a large and costly workforce to ensure that this could be achieved. This was another speculative venture and Lok had no funds to pay for it. Another 20 per cent surcharge was put on investors. This meant that for those who had invested £100, they now owed another £40, all within a space of a few months. For those like Burghley and Warwick, the money was unlikely to be a problem, as they were wealthy men. For others lower down the chain, inability to pay would mean they would lose all of the entitlements that had been agreed beforehand. As Lord Treasurer, Burghley began to do some calculations of his own. He was keen to see the maximum return on his investments and had no reason to doubt the information Lok and Frobisher had given him. He calculated it would take 200 miners 1 month to mine 200 tons of ore. This became the new target. The assays continued into February 1578. Frobisher's temperament got the better of him at this point. Eager to get to sea, he attacked Schutz at his labours in William Wynter's house. The official version in the State Papers reads: '[Frobisher] went to Tower Hill, where, finding Jonas naked at his works and very sick, almost to death, of infection of the smoke of the minerals, he reviled him and drew his dagger on him for not having finished his works.'[9] This was enough for Schutz, whose results were justifiably poor and he withdrew from joining the third expedition.

In March 1578, the Privy Council gave the go ahead for this third voyage. Although there were doubts as to the ore's real value, they were hopeful that the outcome would be favourable. Lok suggested results had been poor due to the inefficiency of the small furnaces used to date and put much stock in his 'great works'. As a thorough and cautious financier, his words were probably enough to convince many investors. This time, the voyage was to be no small-scale venture. The fleet, which had been resting at anchor for over six months, needed repairs. The mining team would need to be bigger to excavate larger quantities of ore, so more vessels would be required. The decision had been made to set up a colony so that all-year-round mining could take place, seasons determined, relations developed with local inhabitants as well as a mindful eye kept on discovering the route to Cathay. It was decided the fleet should number ten vessels in all.

Frobisher as captain-general was charged with running the *Ayde* at his own expense, in return for admiralty over the lands he colonized. He went a step further and commissioned four more vessels, although he charged these to the Cathay Company. On his return, Frobisher was accused of embezzling funds such as dead men's pay and selling arms. Many other military commanders before and since have been accused of similar financial chicanery. His charging the Cathay Company for these four vessels without their knowledge gives credence to these accusations, although he was never brought to book. Michael Lok showed willing, by commissioning a fifth vessel, creating a fleet of fifteen ships. A total of £8,500 was needed to equip the enterprise.

The bill for these huge increases fell to the investors once more – an astronomical 135 per cent surcharge was added. This was too rich even for the company's chief advocate. Lok sold a thousand of his shares to the Duke of Oxford, clearly in an attempt to cut his losses. He had been the major investor, putting up the money for the first two voyages himself. Lok was a shrewd man, but his need to be in control proved to be his undoing. He had, at the commission's behest, been signing all bills and expenses in his own name. When the penny dropped in the following year, he had set himself up as the perfect scapegoat. When the fleet was ready to sail from Harwich in 1578, investments and debts stood at about £8,000,000 in today's figures.

A list of the ships involved in this venture, still the largest fleet to explore the Arctic, is reproduced below:

The *Ayde* – Captain-general Martin Frobisher
The *Thomas Allen* – Vice-admiral Yorke
The *Judith* – Lieutenant-general Edward Fenton
The *Anne Francis* – Captain George Best
The *Hopewell* – Captain Henry Carew
The *Beare* – Captain Richard Filpot
The *Thomas of Ipswich* – Captain William Tanfield
The *Emanuell of Exeter* – Captain Courtney
The *Francis of Foy* – Captain Moyles
The *Moone* – Captain Upcot
The *Busse* – Captain Newton
The *Salamon of Weymouth* – Captain Hugh Randall
The *Dennis* – Captain Kendall
The *Gabriel* – Captain Edmund Harvey
The *Michael* – Captain Matthew Kinnersley [Kyndersley][10]

The list of the ship's company for the *Ayde* has survived. Frobisher as captain-general was to be paid £1 a day, backdated to the previous September. What might be regarded as his staff of officers all received £5 a month. Gilbert Yorke was Frobisher's number two, styled captain; Edward Sellman, Lok's man, was a merchant; Robert Kyndersley was a gentleman; Thomas Thornton was purser; Gregory Bona was gold finer, responsible for the ore; and there was to be a preacher 'to go with Master Frobisher', unnamed in the State Papers.

The long-suffering Christopher Hall was pilot, with crewmen variously listed as sailors or gunners. There were three ship's boys – John Ardington, John Hall and John Thorne, who would have been about 12 years old. Specialists included: another gold finer, William Humfrey; Robert Denham, a goldsmith; there were four carpenters and a pump maker, Thomas Jenkins. John Williams was first mate and John Harwood was surgeon. There were also two trumpeters, Christopher Jackson and Anthony Fisher, who were not on board to entertain but to sound their trumpets as a signalling system, ship to ship or ship to shore.

The total crew now numbered 400, 100 of whom were to stay as colonists, including miners, assayists and chaplains. In the meantime, those who went on the first and second voyages, irrespective of whether they had signed up for the third, were given payment. The lists have survived in the State Papers and make interesting reading. One of the sailors, John White, was taken on at the beginning of April but died at Blackwall on 3 May before the fleet even left port. Andrew Dyer, whose name was given to the Sound in Meta Incognita, was paid £5 but did not sail; no reason is given. His 'boy', Harry Hethersay, stayed behind too. John Brown 'being hurt in the service' was paid £1 6s 8d and discharged. The sailor-gunner William Coombes and carpenter Simon Dee ran away, despite the promise of £1 13s 4d as pay. Fenton received £100, Yorke, Best and Philpot £50. Henry Carew, John Dee, Matthew Kyndersley, Edmond Stafford, William Tanfield, Thomas Chamberlain, Francis Brackenbury, Edmund Harvey, Abraham Linche, Dionysus Settle, Robert Kyndersley, Henry Kirkman and Luke Gwido received £25 each.

This group were the gentleman–adventurers. The rest received payment for specific work. Christopher Hall, as pilot, got £50. Charles Jackman, James Beare, Andrew Dyer and Nicholas Chancellor had gone on both voyages and received £25. Richard Cox and Nicholas Conger had captured the Inuit and got the same. Thomas Boydell and James Wallis were given £25 in compensation because they had been 'maimed by the country people'.[11] Also aboard the fleet for the third voyage were the raw materials for building a settlement, brick and timber as well as iron, glazed tiles and bellows for building furnaces.

The third voyage is a story of arrogance, individual endeavour and complacency. The five accounts available tell the same story but from very different stand points. Hall and Fenton set forth simple ship's logs. Best, even though he had his own command, presents Frobisher the champion. Thomas Ellis puts forward his own individual diary, full of the wonders of the landscape and the excitement of being on such a voyage. Edward Sellman, Lok's representative aboard the *Ayde*, delights in chronicling Frobisher's violence of temper, outbursts of frustration and mistakes. This is hardly surprising, as Frobisher had essentially ruined his employer. Sellman delivered his report to Lok in October, but, since it happened after their return, did not include the fact that Frobisher pulled a knife on Sellman and 'nearly cleave his head' with it.

The voyage began promisingly. Thomas Ellis's account, opening with a particularly awful poem by Abraham Fleming, contains a gushing preface. He admits to being 'not of the best learned or ablest' but merely a sailor 'more studied and used in my Chart and Compass'.[12] Sellman, by comparison, dives straight in – 'Edward Sellman wrote this booke and he delivered it to Michael Lok 2 October, 1578, in London'[13] – and we are away. The *Ayde* and the *Gabriel*, with Hall and Robert Davis as masters, left Bristol on 2 May and took the miners on board at Plymouth four days later, joining the rest of the fleet at Harwich on 31 May.

On 6 June, they sighted Cape Clear and put in at the Irish coast where Sellman wrote to Lok of the progress so far. The previous day, the fleet sighted a Bristol-bound barque that had been attacked by two French men-of-war and had lost five of their company. Such piracy, of course, was common in every sea off Europe – the English as guilty as everyone else – but Frobisher felt sorry for the crew and gave them enough biscuits, cheese, butter and peas to get them home.

The fleet reached Greenland at midnight on 19/20 June. Ellis wrote: '[It] is a very high and cragged land . . . being almost cleane covered with snowe . . . there might we also perceive great isles of ice lying upon the seas like mountains'.[14] For the first time on Friseland, or Greenland, the English made it ashore, although there was no attempt to set up a colony there. The next day, they discovered a good mooring place for their ships, which they named Luke's Sound: 'by reason of one Luke Ward that went with him [Frobisher] a land'.[15] They also came across an Inuit settlement, abandoned except for a couple of dogs which they took with them. Ellis commented on the box of nails they found there, believing that the natives either had 'artificers' amongst them or traded with a superior culture. Sellman reported that Frobisher ordered nothing other than the dogs was to be taken away and that the general believed these natives to be more refined than the Inuit that had been encountered the previous year. They named the island they found West England and the nearby headland Frobisher's Foreland. Much of the ice that Sellman had seen on the last voyage had gone. Without the covering of ice and snow, the land would have looked less forbidding, with bright patches of lichen and heather giving colour to the otherwise grey landscape.

This was a good portent for the rest of the journey, but luck would have it otherwise as on 2 July the fleet reached the mouth of Frobisher Bay and the thick fog that came down made every crewman on every vessel feel like they were the only humans on earth. Barely able to see the bows of their ships, they tried to communicate with each other through the usual ship-to-ship signalling methods of trumpet calls and the beating of drums. The sea was a patchwork of white as the ice floes descended into the mouth of the bay. A change in wind direction, coming from the south-east, caused the ice to advance, an army of winter trapping and separating the vessels from one another. Kendall's *Dennis* struck an iceberg and sank – 'and there perished', Sellman wrote. 'The Bark *Dionyse*,' Ellis wrote, 'being but a weak shippe and bruised afore among the ice, being so leake that she could no longer tarrie above the water, sank.'[16] Though no hands were lost – 'God be thanked', wrote Ellis, its cargo of timber intended for the building of a fort sank beneath the waves.

The ice gripped the sides of the ships. Sails and timber intended for building were lashed to their sides to stop the stranglehold of the freezing seas. 'So that we were faine to ease the ship's sides,' wrote a panic-stricken Ellis, 'from the great and dreary [terrifying] strokes of the ice. Some capstan bars, some fending off with oars, some with planks of two ynches thick, which were broken immediately with the force of the ice.' The eerie sound of creaking bows, splintering wood and shifting ice filled the mariners' ears. 'Thus continued we,' Ellis wrote, 'all that dismal and lamentable night . . . looking for instant death, but our God . . . in the morning he caused the winds to cease and the fog which all that night lay on the face of the water, to clear'.[17]

After two days, the fleet had been split into three, and none were aware of their surroundings. For days, the *Hopewell*, the *Thomas of Ipswich*, the *Moone*, the *Gabriel*, the *Beare* and *Salamon* were drifting alone in dangerous seas. There was no sun to plot course or position and the thick fog left them as frozen and static as the land and sea around them. Fenton's *Judith* and Kyndersley's *Michael* were trapped on the south side of the bay, but they could neither see nor hear each other. The *Anne Francis*, the *Moone*, *Francis of Foy* and Harvey's *Gabriel*, uncertain of their position in relation to the bay, had stayed in open water. Although they were at the mercy of the waves filled with packs of floating ice, at least they were free and not trapped. The remaining eight vessels including the captain-general's *Ayde* pushed westwards into the thick fog. The four at the mouth of the bay caught sight of them and followed suit. For several days there were glimpses of land. Elizabeth Foreland . . . North Foreland.

By 9 July, Christopher Hall aboard the *Thomas Allen* was concerned enough to risk boarding a pinnace and row through the fog and ice to confer with the captain-general. 'I told him that it was not the Straits . . . and he was presently in a great rage and swore by God's wounds that it was'. Hall, loyal friend and navigator of the previous two voyages, had been on the receiving end of Frobisher's temper for the last time. 'Variance between the general and the master,' Sellman wrote. Hall boarded the *Thomas Allen* and turned eastward, followed by three ships including the *Anne Francis*, captained by Frobisher's only remaining true advocate, George Best – 'They break company,' wrote Sellman, 'willingly and very wilfully'.[18] Best may have admired Frobisher's spirit and tenacity but fancied his chances better with the most experienced and able navigator of the fleet.

The stubborn Frobisher pressed on, unaware in the fog that his loyal contingent had dwindled from twelve to eight vessels. After 200 miles he realized his mistake. He was virtually at the mouth of what was to become Hudson Bay three decades later. Some tried to justify his having travelled so far, including Best, who said had he not been so mindful of his priorities he would have pressed on through the much bigger and more impressive Hudson Strait and doubtless reached Cathay. His support was dwindling, however. Hall had been right and many knew it. Edward Sellman wrote at the time: 'Our master could not be persuaded, but doth still make it to be the North shore.'[19]

Frobisher's cantankerous nature was rubbing off on his crew and his fleet. Sellman wrote of a row that broke out between him and two members of the night watch, Holmes and Hill, who had neglected their duties and nearly caused a collision in the dark at Countess of Warwick Sound. Without backing from Frobisher, even a merchant like Sellman could not rebuke men and get away with it. A similar incident occurred later, when Fenton demanded Frobisher take action against dereliction by the *Ayde*'s boatswain. Frobisher again refused and the two men had a screaming row. Frobisher's mistake had cost the expedition nearly a month by the time the *Ayde* managed to re-enter Frobisher Bay on 30 July. When the flagship successfully passed through ice floes, the other vessels did not follow. There was insubordination amongst the crews. They would rather die on the end of a rope for desertion than continue on the perilous and misguided venture. Despite the *Ayde* having sprung a leak after its anchor bounced off ice into its bows, Frobisher successfully reached Countess of Warwick Sound where he found the *Judith* and the *Michael*.

This was timely indeed, as Edward Fenton, believing him and his companions to be the only survivors, had only determined to stay a few days more before abandoning everything and sailing home. His hands had been tied. He had been on land for almost a fortnight and with no tools, building materials or assayers at his disposal, as they were aboard the rest of the fleet, he could commence neither mining nor building a settlement. His time instead had been spent exploring the interior of the mainland off Countess of Warwick Sound. The sailors of the *Michael* and *Judith* were sent out to the remainder of the fleet, who by now were scattered right along the opposite shore of the bay. They were to guide them safely into Countess of Warwick Sound. This was achieved slowly and tentatively over the next few days. Pinnaces acted as tugs, whilst crew members jumped from the ships' sides physically to push ice floes away from the ships' hulls. Not all the vessels were present. The *Anne Francis*, captained by Best, had lingered at the mouth of the bay for some time, occasionally sighting the *Moone* and *Thomas of Ipswich* in thick fog. The *Thomas of Ipswich*, replete with half the brick intended for the settlement, took advantage of the fog, which saved several captains from punishment, and slipped back to England. The *Anne Francis* pressed into the Bay, with the *Moone* just behind.

In the distance, Best saw an outcrop of black rock. Excellent! A new and very large deposit of ore to mine and to return to England. The *Anne Francis* struck the rocks and was grounded. Best had no ship to continue but he was so lifted at finding land he motioned to sail a pinnace up the coast and find the rest of the fleet. The reality was that the *Anne Francis* had no pinnace, and neither was there wood of sufficient strength to build one, the wood on board having been splintered and cracked whilst protecting the sides from the ice. The determined smith and carpenter made the best pinnace they could and despite the carpenter's serious doubts as to its seaworthiness, Best and around twenty of the crew slowly worked their way towards Countess of Warwick Sound. After three days, on 21 August, they cautiously approached an unknown camp and were relieved to hear English voices. Best provides by far the most eloquent and literate accounts of the voyage, and even with artistic licence this is the primary tale of salvation from the whole expedition.

Back on Countess of Warwick Island the arrival of Frobisher had spurred things into action. He may not have been the idolized leader he once was, but he was ready to push the men. Within a day, 1 August, the miners were at work. A furnace was quickly assembled, attested to by Fenton's recording an assay on the evening of the first day and by the hearth and burned deposits found in excavations of the 1980s. Frobisher called a meeting of the whole company and, as with many who sense dissention, set out some rules. No one could take ore for themselves; no one was to go anywhere other than Countess of Warwick or the neighbouring island of Wynter's Furnace without permission and no one was to draw a weapon or they would lose their right hand. No offences were punishable by death; Frobisher needed every man he had.

The mines of Countess of Warwick Island were soon deemed to be too difficult to work, so it became imperative to find new sites. Some had been identified before and others were discovered by a constant flow of searches along the coast. The weather had begun to settle but the ice gave way to sleet and slush, rain lashing the miners as they worked with temperatures only just above freezing. New sites were found at the Countess of Sussex Mine, Wynter's Furnace (Newland Island), named after the assistant commissioner, Denham's Mount on Judy Point and Fenton's Fortune (Tikkoon's Point). These all lay within a 5–10-mile radius of Countess of Warwick Sound. Even the exhausted Best returned to his ship the day after finding base camp to mine some of the ore he had found. Countess of Warwick Island itself changed from mine to centre of mining activities, leading to the construction of the smithy and Fenton's House.

With the mining underway, Frobisher and his second in command Fenton turned their attention to the settlement. By now, it was mid-August and the death toll began. Sellman wrote: 'God called to his mercy Philip, who had charge of certain apparel brought in by the Generall for the mariners and miners and also one of the bark *Denys*, a man called Trelos, one also of the *Armorell* [*Emanuell of Exeter*] and another out of the *Francis of Foy*, all buryed upon Wynter's Furnace this present day.'[20]

The project was nearly two months in and the mining had been going on for little more than two weeks. It was determined that 60, not a 100 hundred men should be left in the settlement with Fenton as their governor. The names of the original 100 – actually 108 – have survived, but it is not known how they were chosen. Richard Philpot and George Best were to have been Fenton's seconds in command, together with John Dee and Edward Harvey as officers. There were six others listed specifically as gentlemen and ten as soldiers, including Nicholas Conger, who had captured an Inuit on the previous voyage. Mr Woolfall was the preacher, presumably Anglican.

The 'artificers, miners and labourers' included five men listed purely as labourers, three as miners, two as shoemakers and one as a founder. Some of them doubled up; the miner John Heywood was also a cook. The doctors, lumped together with artificers as a reminder of their lowly status in Elizabethan England, were Robert Hind, surgeon of the *Michael*, and John Paradise, surgeon of the *Judith*. There were two bakers, two smiths, two coopers, a fishmonger, a carpenter and a tailor. Nicholas Chancellor was the purser responsible for the stores and as such, drew higher wages than the rest.

There were twenty-one crewmen of the *Judith* led by Charles Jackman with William Ward as first mate. Two of them are listed as gunners and two as shipwrights; the others merely sailors.

The *Michael* was to furnish eleven crewmen under Bartholomew Bull, with first mate William Bennes. All the others were sailors, except boatswain Giles Syllabin and shipwright Harry Spragge.

Thomas Price led the eight-strong contingent of the *Gabriel*, with John Lunt as his number two.

Ellis waxes eloquent on behalf of these men. They possessed, he says, 'most willing hearts, venturous minds, stout stomachs and singular manhood', which implies they were probably volunteers. They were, after all, prepared to weather appalling storms and risk death 'among a barbarous and uncivil people, infidels and miscreants'.[21] And it was merely the loss of the *Dennis* and the apparent disappearance of the *Thomas of Ipswich* that meant they could not stay.

The fort could not be built due to lack of timber and half the brick had been left aboard the *Thomas of Ipswich*. The masons and carpenters protested that they could build a house for forty men at best and that this would take them a further month and a half. Frobisher, therefore, decided to abandon the plan, much to the relief of the prospective settlers, for although they had not wintered there, Frobisher had seen the beginning of seasonal change twice before and knew that the Arctic winter would be even harsher. He instead made arrangements with Fenton for supplies and timber to be buried in readiness for the next voyage, which everyone expected would happen the following year.

Fenton did supervise the building of one stone structure, Fenton's House, the first to be built in the New World. This 'little beginning', as he put it, was a practice run for the colony he would build and govern. Ellis records that they left mementoes behind for the natives: 'pinnes, pointes, laces, glasses, combes, babes on horseback and on foote with innumerable other such fancies and toyes; thereby to allure and entice the people to some familiarity against other yeares'.[22]

But of the Inuit they had seen virtually nothing. This is hardly surprising, based on their abduction of Inuit on the previous two voyages, coupled with the size of the new expedition, four times larger than previously. The English rather optimistically made an

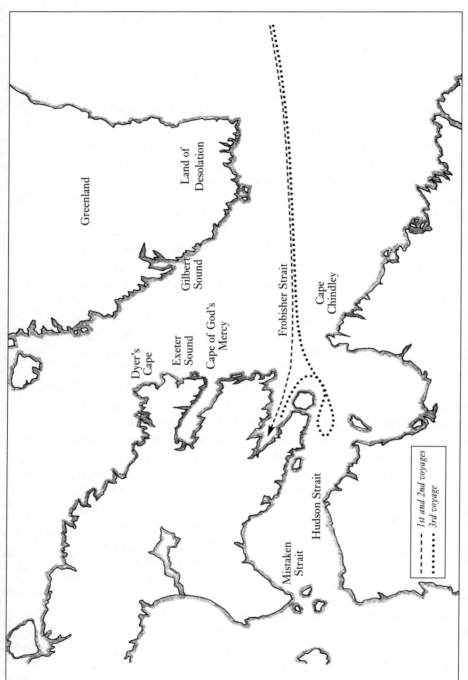

Map showing the three voyages of Martin Frobisher including his attempt to find another way to the Northwest Passage. Ironically, had he continued beyond Mistaken Strait, he would have found what is now Hudson Bay, and perhaps lent his name to a hugely successful trading company!

The following labels appear on the map:

Greenland

Land of Desolation

Gilbert Sound

Dyer's Cape

Exeter Sound

Cape of God's Mercy

Frobisher Strait

Cape Chindley

Hudson Strait

Mistaken Strait

- - - - - 1st and 2nd voyages
········· 3rd voyage

attempt to plant crops in the ravaged, slag-strewn ground of Countess of Warwick Island. The soil of the Canadian Arctic is constantly covered by a layer of permafrost. At best, vegetation in the tundra of Baffin Island sustains moss and small shrubs. European cereals stood no chance.

By the end of August, the sleet and slush had hardened to hail and snow. The men began to take to the ships on the 30th. The chaplain, Thomas Woolfall, held a solemn communion for those still on the island. The approach of a new moon meant that the seas were whipped into a frenzy and embarkation became rushed. Ore was loaded clumsily. Barrels were smashed, losing more of the severely depleted beer stocks, adding to the sailors' despair as they had already lost half even before reaching Countess of Warwick Sound. It soon became a question of every man for himself. A gale began to blow, buffeting ships and washing men and cargo overboard. Surprisingly, only forty men were lost from the whole company, including five buried during the mining and five who died at sea on the return journey. Boats were crammed with too many people and officers were unevenly dispersed amongst the ships as they were smashed by the sea, desperately trying to make it to open water.

Frobisher, keen to load as much ore as possible, risked his life and those of many men and sacrificed several pinnaces and skiffs to the waves. He ended up on board the *Gabriel*, his command from the first voyage and it took four days for them to navigate into open water, abandoning the *Emanuell* and the *Michael*. Thomas Wiars was on board the 'Emanuel, otherwise called the Buss of Bridgewater' under James Leech and left a report of his experiences from the time the ship was left behind in Bear Sound on 2 September. His report is very brief, ending with a sighting of Galway on the 25th, but, oddly, he does not mention the ship's sinking. The *Ayde* returned without the captain's cabin, fortunately not occupied by Frobisher. Many logs and maps had been lost.

The fleet, if it could still be called that, limped back to England in early October 1578. Sellman listed some of the dead on the

grim journey back: 'God called to His mercy Walter Krell and
Thomas Tort . . . Thomas Coningham . . . John Wilmet . . .
Cornelius Rich, a Dutchman'.[23] The sycophantic Thomas Ellis
rounded off his account with sickly verses in praise of Frobisher:
'to our Generall, long life, good health and fortunate succeed, in
all his voyages, to the profit and commodity of our native soil and
countrie'.[24]

The hardships and toil of the voyage were over, but the
troubles had only just begun. Elizabeth's paranoid state
machinery swung into action. All charts, plans and descriptions of
the voyage were to be seized by the government and nothing could
be published. In October, Thomas Bonham, who had spent £300
furnishing the *Thomas of Ipswich*, petitioned the government for
£100 towards repairs of the weather-beaten ship. Bearing in mind
the *Thomas* had turned tail and 'had furtively sailed for England',
this seems the height of cheek.

Over a thousand tons of ore had been successfully transported
back to England, but the Cathay Company was in dire straits. The
money they had levied from the surcharges had all been spent on
the smelting works in Dartford and with two vessels, the *Dennis*
and *Emanuell*, lost at sea and whole stocks of supplies unpaid for,
the creditors began to close in. The Privy Council, under
Elizabeth's auspices, allowed one more surcharge to raise the
necessary £6,000 to keep the company afloat. This must have been
a bitter pill to swallow for even the richest investors and many
refused to pay. On 30 November, a list of these debtors was
compiled. Of those named, six were members of the court,
including Burleigh, Howard of Effingham, the Lord Admiral and
Lord Hunsdon. A number of titled people appear, including
several whose names had been given to barren outcrops of ice far
to the North-West. The Countess of Sussex is there, as is the
Countess of Warwick. John Dee's name is listed, as well as those
of William Bond, Thomas Gresham and the Kyndersley brothers.
Michael Lok owed £450, as did the Earl of Oxford. Even Martin
Frobisher owed £270 for his own voyage! The total in arrears was
£4,115 10s. Walsingham had been forced to pay nearly £400 more

than he had expected. The proviso was simple: get the ore refined and count the gold. As the Privy Council put it, aware of the fiery-haired Queen's fiery temperament, 'her Majestie hathe very great expectation of the same'.

So the ore was rushed to Dartford and the refining process began. Trials in November and December were not promising. Though gold and silver were obtained, they were of negligible amounts. When assays were successful, it transpired that the additives used in the process were the source of the precious metal. When the ore was valued at a loss of £10 some sought to blame the refining process, none more so than Frobisher, who, with a company of forty men, launched into a physical tirade against Lok and Schutz. There was no longer any love lost between captain and financier.

It seems as if Frobisher was upsetting everybody. On 13 January, Thomas Allen wrote to Walsingham: 'Mr Frobisher much misuses him in words . . . Sir, he will weary us all and he have the bridle too much.'[25] And Allen insisted that Frobisher's books be checked.

Lok's attack on Frobisher runs to four closely written pages in the State Papers. He failed to bring enough ore back from the second and third voyages and the value of it was negligible. He added four ships and a hundred crew beyond the parameters laid down by the commission. He failed to give Fenton any real power 'and feared that Fenton's deeds would dash his own glory' and also failed to leave the colony behind 'because he disliked that enterprice'.[26] He did not find a passage through to Cathay; Hall and Jackman were available to testify to that. He skimped on the *Ayde*'s stores, which resulted in the deaths of crewmen. He obtained cash for miners' clothing and equipment, which they never received. He 'led all the ships to a wrong place through his obstinate ignorance'[27] – and Hall, Davis and the other masters would corroborate that. At Dartford, he drew his dagger on Captain Fenton and would have 'mischiefed' him if other officers had not calmed him down. 'He is so full of lying talk as no man may credit anything he doth speak and so impudent of his tongue as his best friends are most slandered of him when he cannot have his will.'[28]

The crew of the *Ayde* behaved badly at the ship's Thames anchorage, bringing the Cathay Company into disrepute. Lok's account of the voyages was written after things had turned sour and it is through this bitter relationship that we hear most of Frobisher's temper. It is documented elsewhere, however, so we know that Lok was not just writing out of spite. Lok's four pages, which seem to prove that the man had a point, were answered by the less than literate Frobisher in four lines:

> [Lok] hath made false accounts to the Companye and hath cossened [cheated] them of £3000 of money.
>
> He hath cossened my Lord of Oxford of £1000.
>
> He hath not one groat [a small coin, worth 4*d*] of venture in these voyages.
>
> He is a bankerot [bankrupt] knave.[29]

Ironically, the only true point in the above was the last one, and that through no fault of Lok's.

By January 1579, the ore's value had dropped to £5 a ton and by February was deemed worthless. The assets such as they were of the Cathay Company were sold to pay off debts or taken in lieu of payment. The *Gabriel*, for example, the only vessel to take part in all three voyages, was sold for a paltry £60. Michael Lok, now a ruined man, was removed as head of the Cathay Company in December 1578 and as sole signatory for much of the expenditure saw the inside of a debtor's prison no less than seven times, his creditors pursuing him into the next century. In January 1579 he petitioned the Privy Council to try to make good some of his losses. He had paid out over £6,000 'whereby himself, his wife and 15 children are left to beg their bread henceforth'.[30] His only hope, if the Council was not listening (and it was not), was 'except God turn the stones at Dartford into his bread again'.[31] The Council's answer to all this was to doubt whether Lok spent anything like this amount on the three voyages and pointing up the fact that he and Frobisher had been friends and that the previously broke Frobisher had been treated very generously by Lok. The Yorkshireman had lodged at Mr Brown's house in Fleet Street, then at Widow Hancock's in Mark Lane, largely at Lok's expense whilst Frobisher worked tirelessly with him to make the voyages a reality. The rest of the Council's answer was a brief outline of the voyages, how Frobisher had returned with 'his strange man of Cathay' and became the darling of the court. None of this really eased Lok's predicament and he gave up.

Despite this, he never lost his love for discovery and expansion, even toying with the dream of an expedition to find the North-West Passage when he was living in Venice in the 1590s, well into his sixties. The ore lay by the disused mill at Dartford and can now be seen in a wall near Dartford station. Its only useful worth at the time was ironically against the English; the cargo from the sunk *Emanuell* was used by Irish rebels to build a defensive position for Spanish and French soldiers in the 1580s.

The financial disasters of the Frobisher voyages are tempered in history by their effect on the English. They promoted entrepreneurialism, they made the world bigger, they fed a hunger for the new and the unfamiliar. They made England want to become the British Empire. In 1577 Drake left Plymouth, circumnavigating the globe and returning in 1580 with a vast fortune. Sir Walter Ralegh founded the first English colony in the New World at Roanoke in 1585 and though it did not survive, by 1607 there was a permanent settlement in Jamestown, Virginia.

What of Frobisher? He had expected a knighthood for his services on the voyages, but the whole thing had left a nasty taste and he would have to wait until his time against the Armada for the accolade. He became involved in Leicester's expedition in 1582 to round the Cape of Good Hope but did not go to sea, having either declined or been refused command of the expedition, the position going to Edward Fenton who he no longer counted as a friend. He was now living in the shadow of other men. His voyages had cost Queen, country and investor almost £10,000,000 by modern standards, with no return. The hero of the hour, Sir Francis Drake, had spent £2,000,000 setting up his fabled voyage of 1577, returning with an astonishing £2.5 billion, enough to pay off Elizabethan England's national debt. It must have pained Frobisher to be under the command of Drake, both in the West Indies and against the Armada, a man who had succeeded so brilliantly where he had failed.

What Martin Frobisher had done in searching for the North-West Passage to China, in mining fool's gold in the inhospitable North and in bringing back to England his 'strange man of Cathay' was to introduce to the civilized world of Europe a new people – the Inuit.

Chapter 8

In the Shadow of Giants

In 1581 the scholar Thomas Smith expounded the virtues of gold in his *Discourse of the Common Weal of this Realm of England*. Apart from its obvious natural beauty, gold was portable, effecting an easier exchange system than simply bartering like for like, for example wool for grain. It removed the necessity for trading nations to carry large cargoes in the hope of engaging in commerce. Gold was ageless, not being affected or ravaged by the passage of time. It could be divided and then melted down and joined together. With no markets or exchange rates pertaining to gold, the promise of its existence was enough. This was to prove the case during the Frobisher voyages, although they concluded unsuccessfully. In his second voyage to Roanoke, Sir Walter Ralegh was even more blatant, asking for finance in return for gold he promised was available although he had no proof of this. At least Frobisher maintained the gold standard by returning with his ore.

'Inevitably it was the gold and silver of the New World which most attracted the attention of 16th century Europeans.'[1] Spain, and to a lesser extent Portugal, controlled the vast majority of the flow of precious metals from the New World. This had been seen only too clearly in England with the procession of Philip's dowry to Queen Mary, which included twenty-seven chests of bullion and ninety-seven boxes of silver. Other European monarchs were also interested in the riches available in these new territories, as evidenced in a letter from Francis I of France to Charles V of Spain 'Your Majesty and the King of Portugal have divided the world between you, offering no part of it to me. Show me, I pray you, the will of our father Adam, so that I may see that he has made you his only universal heirs.'[2]

By the reign of Elizabeth, Spain was beginning to resent its position as the richest nation in Europe. It had since the 1560s endured continued attacks from the Low Countries, France and England. No Spanish cargo was safe and Philip's patience was wearing thin. He began to try to curb trade between his interests in the New World and his European neighbours. During the 1560s, John Hawkins, son of William, began to form relationships with the Spanish and Portuguese colonies in the New World. This was via the medium of the slave trade.

Slavery had existed amongst the West African tribes for generations and the Arabs were the first to capitalize on it. As European explorers sailed both the African coasts and those of the New World, they realized that the African mindset and physical strength was superior to that of the indigenous Arawaks and Caribs of the West Indies. The transporting of slaves was the obvious solution. Amongst the English, Hawkins was undoubtedly the most successful of the slave traders, and the fact that this devoutly religious man treated slaves like cattle should not be seen as a dichotomy. It would be two and a half centuries before Britain abolished the slave trade and three before America followed suit, at the cost of the bloodiest war in its history.

Hawkins became a wealthy man through these ventures, but in mainland Spain he was mistrusted and the Spaniards were wary of giving him too much freedom. The clearest example of this was his furnishing two ships with sugar, fine cloth and wine from the Azores, which he had purchased with profits from selling slaves around the West Indies. These two ships he sent to the Spanish markets, where they were seized as contraband because the ships and their cargo were not Spanish. Hawkins was harried at every turn. In 1564, he was fired upon in the West Indies, officials mistaking him for a privateer. This was erroneous but hardly surprising as the vast majority of non-Spanish ships in these waters were there to plunder. In 1567 during a third slave-trading voyage, Hawkins reached the Caribbean with his cargo of slaves. These had been particularly hard to procure and after a stormy crossing that had seen his fleet scattered, he was somewhat aggrieved to find that nobody would trade with him.

A favourite at court, Hawkins had been invited to dinner by the ambassador of Spain. This was to keep public face and international relations secure at a time when the major powers of Europe were involved in the diplomacy of avoiding war. Hawkins' tales of illegal trade and anti-Spanish stance at this dinner caused the Spanish ambassador to write to Philip who, outraged, informed his governors in the New World not to conduct trade with him. At Rio de la Hacha, Hawkins found his entry to the port barred. The cannonets that guarded the gates opened fire and Hawkins, fuelled by anger and in the knowledge that there were those in the port who would wish to purchase his cargo, smashed his vessels through the gates. Fearful of the man who was fast gaining a reputation as a terrible pirate from their homeland, the Spanish garrison retreated into the town and Hawkins was successful in selling much of his cargo. Hostages were, however, taken from both sides and a climate of detente ensued. Against his better judgement, Hawkins left his hostages and sailed to Vera Cruz to continue his now illicit trade. There he was ambushed by a Spanish fleet operating in those waters and a pitched sea battle was fought.

The Spanish flagship and two others were sunk, but Hawkins only narrowly escaped with two vessels, the *Minion* under his command and the *Judith* under the command of a young Francis Drake. This was the final straw for both countries and the walls of diplomacy began to crumble. Hawkins, always loyal to the Crown, was quite a devious character. In 1571, he offered to defect to the Spanish cause if his crewmen who were held hostage were returned and if he was paid for his losses. The Spaniards, eager to have a man of

Hawkins' calibre on their side and doubtless mindful of clawing back a semblance of international relations, agreed. Hawkins, however, had turned the tables; from information he gained whilst 'working' for the Spaniards, he was instrumental in uncovering the Ridolfi Plot, the first in a series of Spanish-backed attempts to place Mary, Queen of Scots, on the throne of England. Briefly told, the plot was hatched in response to the failed rebellion against Elizabeth by northern Catholics. Mary, Queen of Scots, still remained the Queen's prisoner and the Pope published his edict *Regnans in Excelsis*, which amounted to a hitman's charter against Elizabeth. Roberto Ridolfi, a Florentine banker living in England, believed that a rising backed by 10,000 Catholic troops under the Duke of Alva would be successful. Hawkins' close association with the Spanish ambassador, Guerau de Spes, led to his discovery of the plot which he was quick to pass on to the Privy Council.

In 1583, Spain had almost completely subjugated neighbouring Portugal. Lisbon had fallen in 1580 with eleven Portuguese galleons joining the ever-growing Spanish fleet. In the same year, Admiral Santa Cruz had effectively wiped out Portuguese influence in the Azores. Meanwhile, in England, Spain had become public enemy number one, with support for religious wars in France and the subjugation of the Irish taking second place. The Throckmorton Plot between Philip and Mary, Queen of Scots, had been uncovered and was fast pushing the Elizabethan war machine into action. Francis Throckmorton was intercepted as go-between in another attempt to assassinate the Queen. The plan was to link this with an invasion by Henri, Duke of Guise, from France and to install Mary, Queen of Scots, on the English throne. Walsingham's spy network and his methods of interrogation first revealed then broke Throckmorton, who was executed for treason in 1584.

A plot was one thing, but there was still a great fear of open war between any of Europe's major powers. The Netherlands would doubtless have allied with England in view of the latter's support in the Dutch revolt, and especially after the Spanish assassination of William of Orange. William of Nassau – 'the silent' – had been the leader of the Protestant revolt of the Netherlands. Philip had placed a price of 25,000 crowns on his head. A Frenchman, Balthasar Gerard, attempted to claim it when he engineered a private audience with William at his house in Delft and shot him with a pistol in the chest at point-blank range. Gerard's execution in July 1584 was amongst the most ghastly witnessed in a very bloody century.

The case for France was not so clear, for although at sea France and Spain attacked each other and took prisoners, English involvement in the Huguenot uprisings meant that French Catholic sympathizers, which included the Crown, would most likely side with Spain.

In 1585, Philip was a man in need, however. A poor harvest meant that English trade was necessary to make up his agricultural shortfall. The merchants of England sent a fleet into the port of Bilbao. They had been duped. Philip had come to the decision that he was no longer to be the target of international privateering and with a vast fleet in port and being built in Cadiz he decided now was his time to act. He seized the merchant fleet taking its ships, cargo and crew. The vessel that reported this, the *Primrose*, had a large part to play in what followed and was captained by none other than Martin Frobisher.

How had a man disgraced and branded a failure seven years earlier found himself in command of a ship of the line? The answer is that Frobisher did what he did best, he volunteered to patrol dangerous waters for his Queen and country; in those years, the waters were the Irish Sea. The *Primrose* had been purchased and commissioned in 1560 and at 800 tons was one of the two largest ships in the Queen's fleet (the other was the *Victory*). She carried forty-three guns, firing various weights of shot and had been decommissioned in 1575, which may well explain how Frobisher became her captain.

Whilst Drake was earning glory sailing the world, the on-going threat to the country remained from Philip's and the

Pope's machinations in Ireland. James Fitzgerald gained support from Munster and even discontented Catholics in the English Pale around Dublin. Ireland in open rebellion would provide the clichéd springboard for invasion from the west which Philip could find invaluable should open warfare break out. By November 1580, Fitzgerald's rebellion had been brutally crushed, with massive loss of life and forfeiture of lands. Fitzgerald himself, on the run, was finally captured and killed in November 1583.

Early in the next year, Sir John Perrott, a former Lord Admiral, was made Lord Deputy in Ireland, with the unenviable task of keeping the lid on Anglo–Irish tensions. The Irish had no fleet of their own, of course, but Frobisher would have been concerned to watch out for Spanish, Portuguese or French merchantmen slipping into Irish harbours for fear of what men and arms they might be carrying.

After his actions in Bilbao, Philip put out a commission to seize any Dutch, English or French vessel. Diplomacy had failed. Sir Francis Drake, who had returned home a hero from his circumnavigation of the globe in 1580, had since that time been petitioning the Queen to allow him to harry the Spanish at sea. In 1582 and 1583 there had been movements towards this. The Earl of Leicester had begun preparations for English vessels to operate in the West Indies and Africa but these preparations had been slow and unsuccessful. By 1585, with any hope of avoiding conflict gone, Drake and his fellow mariners were given carte blanche to attack and seize Spanish ships and cargoes wherever they found them. And so Drake, who had been waiting for this opportunity, began to formulate a plan of how best this was to be effected. He maintained that although attacking the Spanish wherever he found them would be effective, he recognized the importance of striking at the source of Spain's wealth, the New World.

Although the provenance is unknown, a campaign plan does survive for Drake's actions in the West Indies. By the end of the year, he intended to have sacked several significant ports, including Rio de la Hacha, Marguerita, capital of what is now the Dominican Republic, and Santo Domingo in Hispaniola. He also proposed to hold the administrative capital of Cartagena to ransom, suggesting that it would levy a huge sum of 1 million ducats or, at about 6*d* a ducat, £25,000 (£1,000,000 in today's currency). By the end of March the following year, he planned to have taken Havana, Panama and conducted significant crippling raids along the coast of Honduras. The reality was very different. Little is known of Frobisher's thoughts on Drake, although in later years he was quick to speak harshly of Drake's self-obsession and seize on his apparent mistakes. Rather than creating a narrative concerning the greatest hero of the Elizabethan age and, therefore, perhaps overshadow our main protagonist, it will serve to highlight Drake as the man he was, undoubtedly an able tactician, but also a man given over to his emotions in favouring certain men over others, impulsive and at times reckless.

The best-known account of Drake's West Indian expedition (the Spanish use of the term raids is more accurate) comes from Walter Bigges, the captain of a company of Foot who was killed at Cartagena. On his death, Bigges' narrative was taken up by Lieutenant Croftes and the whole thing put together (in Latin and English) under the title *A Summarie and True Discourse of Sir Francis Drake's West Indian Voyage* in 1589 by editor Thomas Cates, who dedicated the book to the Earl of Essex.

Drake's fleet consisted of around 30 vessels (Bigges says 25); 11 ships, 3 barques and about 20 pinnaces. There was also a combined land and sea force of around 2,500 men, a force of military might. Amongst the ships was the *Ayde*, Frobisher's erstwhile flagship. Drake was aboard the vast *Elizabeth Bonaventure*. This impressive 600-tonner had been commissioned in 1567 and remained in service until 1611. Her deck rails were painted a striking black and white and she carried the royal arms on her stern and a red dragon, the Welsh emblem of the Tudors, on her beak head. The two most important ships after this were the *Leicester*, sometimes known as *Lettice Leicester*, and the *Primrose*, both 400 tons, by far the biggest in the fleet. The *Leicester* was under the command of Elizabeth's cousin, Francis Knollys, who acted as rear admiral. The *Primrose* was under the command of the fleet's vice-admiral, Martin Frobisher. Bigges noted of Frobisher, 'a man most experienced of sea matters', and in that one line probably encapsulated the future animosity between Frobisher and Drake. Initially, Drake was highly complimentary of his commanders, eager to engender a 'brotherhood' of command. Frobisher and the fleet's lieutenant-general in charge of its land force, Christopher Carleill – 'a man' wrote Bigges 'most experienced in war by land and sea', joined Drake aboard his ship as it set sail. 'Above all men elce, and with all requiringe in frendly sorte to be advartysed by us of anythinge which we coulde wyshe to have altered or amended . . .'

With the exception of Carleill, a clear favourite of Drake, this turned out to be far from the case. The capture of Spanish vessels at sea commenced immediately and the English began in home waters. On 24 September, Frobisher captured seven grain ships filled with Spanish salt with only one pinnace. Drake purchased one of these, *La Madeleine*, changing its name to *Drake* and adding it to the fleet. This may well have annoyed Frobisher, who had brought back the richest spoil to date and as a man eager to gain recognition was left with neither acknowledgement nor spoils of his own. There can be little doubt that Frobisher saw this expedition as a chance to shine and re-ingratiate himself at court. Such a brilliant start for him personally deserved mention and he could not be sure how generous Drake was when it came to despatches.

By early October, having put in to the two rather alarmed Spanish coastal towns of Bayonne and Vigo, the governors of which asked Carleill whether their respective countries were at war, the raiding party moved eastward. Bigges was delighted to receive what amounted to blackmail money from these governors who had hurried down to the ships with wine, oil, grapes and 'marmalade (thus they call a sweet delicacy)'.

Storms blew up as the fleet set off. The *Talbot* was driven back to England, damaged, and the *Hawkins* and the *Speedwell* managed to right themselves and catch up. Drake split the fleet into two, half under his command and half under Frobisher. This was to spread the effectiveness of their raids. The fleet largely operated together, however, except when bad weather forced them to separate. The bad luck that was to haunt this endeavour began on 28 October when Drake learned from the crew of a large, armed French merchantmen that Philip's richest prize, his treasure fleet, had already passed through several days before. Drake was further frustrated when on reaching Palma in the Canaries on 30 October the coastal batteries effectively repelled the English fleet. Putting into the Isla de Ferro, 1,000 of Carleill's troops disembarked, waiting in formation in the foothills of a mountain range. The terrified locals brought a young English resident to talk to Carleill and he assured the general that the island was virtually destitute. Realizing this was true, Drake and Frobisher sailed on, putting in at the African coast at Cabo Bianco.

Here the crews had time to fish and dined on the splendid beaches with a small French war fleet anchored in the same place. It was not until 17 November on reaching Santiago in the Cape Verde Islands that the fleet tasted success. Bigges records that 1,000 footsoldiers disembarked under Carleill and they marched through rugged countryside in the dark. Finding an open plain before Santiago at dawn, they were deployed in open formation in three 'battles' (units). The town was built on low ground and Captains Sampson and Barton, with thirty musketeers each, reconnoitred the area.

With no opposition at all, they raised the cross of St George on the city's seaward side so that Drake and Frobisher, riding at anchor offshore, could see that the place had been taken.

The 17th was no ordinary day. It was the anniversary of the Queen's coronation and Carleill commanded that every one of the city's fifty cannon be fired in commemoration. Drake and Frobisher answered gun for gun, the smoke drifting across the shore and the sky ringing to the cheers of soldiers and sailors. Crucially in this period, sailors and soldiers were not autonomous. Land forces could be as much at home in the rigging as on a battlefield and vice versa. However, divisions, particularly between officers, were one of the main problems that dogged this expedition.

Christopher Carleill was an experienced soldier having been involved in the Dutch revolt under Henry Morgan in 1573 and in France fighting for the Huguenots in 1577. He shared common ground with Frobisher through his involvement with the Muscovy Company. To begin with, it had been co-founded by his grandfather, Sir George Barne, Lord Mayor of London. Carleill had been employed by the company to protect English ships travelling north-east as the Russian tsar, Ivan IV, was locked in an ongoing war with Frederick II of Denmark. He gained fame and recognition for successfully repelling the Danish fleet, which was emerging as a significant naval power. His ambitions went beyond soldiery and through his knowledge of exploration he had tried to gain sponsorship to set up a colony near Cape Breton Island in North America, although this plan never came to fruition. It is also interesting to note that his stepfather was Francis Walsingham, who, as has been seen, was more than keen to invest in such commercial ventures.

Drake's troops stayed at Santiago for two weeks. There was no trouble from the townsfolk who were no doubt glad to give them presents of wine, oil, vinegar and wheat just to see them go. Striking a slightly alarmist note, Bigges wrote: 'but there was nothing of gold or silver nor anything else of significant value'. On the 24th they pushed on with 600 troops to Santo Domingo, some 30 miles from the sea and too far for Frobisher's big guns to help them. The place was deserted, the locals hiding in the hills. As Carleill marched back, they appeared 'with horse and foot', as Bigges put it, in other words, ready for battle, but no shots were fired.

Whilst Frobisher supervised the disembarkation of the land forces, the last remaining torched the city, having helped themselves to the only two cannon stashed away that they could find. The fleet sailed at 6 o'clock that evening.

It was about this time that the murmurings began. An unnamed officer, whose journal survives from the *Leicester*, writes of Drake's inconsistencies and his choosing of favourites, particularly Carleill. Santiago had been a successful but not very profitable victory and dissention was never very far away. Perhaps sensing this, in a rather confused and undiplomatic manner, Drake decided he wanted his entire command to declare oaths of loyalty. As Bigges put it: 'Each captain conducted a muster of his troops, who took an oath of loyalty under death towards her royal majesty of England as their supreme mistress and that they would always obey the orders of their General and his officers.' This was an odd move, evidenced by the fact that Bigges mentioned it at all. First, it was halfway through the journey and, secondly, captains far more intelligent than Drake would have seen this as the decision of a worried man. Despite this, all of the commanding officers signed, apart from Francis Knollys. The conflict between Knollys and Drake was far from a secret and has its origins here.

Sir Francis Knollys had come to court under Henry VIII. He was son of Anne Boleyn's sister, Mary, and therefore a cousin of the Queen. From an early age he was drawn to politics and had been Elizabeth's guardian over Mary, Queen of Scots. Though mindful of a French and Spanish alliance, he had been pleased when the Queen saw sense to move against Spain. His sister, Lettice Dudley, married Robert Dudley, Earl of Leicester, hence the name of his ship, *Lettice Leicester*.

Knollys was powerful, intelligent and stubborn. His dislike of Drake sprang from a number of quarters. Carleill had been given command of organizing the watch and living accommodation for the English in Santiago. Deliberately favouring his land officers, Knollys, Frobisher (although he remained silent) and other sea captains found their crews standing watch for a number of days or even removed from their command completely in favour of Carleill's soldiers. Secondly, he was unwilling to confer total control to Drake, as he possibly doubted his ability to command. The third reason is a religious one. Knollys was a devout puritan, thinking that Elizabeth's reintroduction of the Protestant church in England did not go far enough. He was, however, wholly opposed to the militant actions of the extreme religious left. Drake and Carleill were Calvinists and their destruction of the churches in Santiago would have been abhorrent to Knollys. Whilst at a conference of all the captains on board ship, Knollys and Drake openly argued with one another, culminating in Drake confining him to the *Leicester*. The matter was left unresolved until a few months later when Drake pleaded with him to sign the oath and Knollys still refused.

Knollys was put aboard the pinnace *Hawkins* and was intended to sail home in disgrace. However, he ended up remaining with the fleet as rear admiral. One or both of the men had backed down. It is possible it was Drake, realizing by this point that Knollys was not acting out of mutinous desires but out of pride. In Elizabethan times, courts martial were a rarity. The first and only example at sea is in 1587 when the crew of the *Golden Lion* abandoned their position at Cadiz. Even then, their defence proved justifiable as the crews on land and at sea were so near to starvation that their situation had become untenable. Martial law was rarely applied at sea. It could only be approved by the Crown and even then the actions of commanders were invariably answerable when they returned home. Drake had powers of martial law, as did John Lok when operating in Guinea, though neither of the men chose to use it as sea captains were ever mindful of their relations with their crew. Mariners were loyal and followed orders, but only whilst those orders made sense and whilst they trusted their commanders, favouring experience over high birth. Frobisher's experience in the Arctic bears this out.

There his men put up with many privations, backing him until the situation became so serious that they had to speak out, preventing him from sailing into unknown territory in Hudson Bay when he had believed himself to be off Countess of Warwick Island.

Bigges noted with horror the plague that hit the fleet off the West Indies and killed more than 300 men. Having left Santiago eight days previously, the only loss of life they had encountered was a ship's boy, who had been caught, decapitated and disembowelled by the locals. Now, the threat was of 'a dry fever', weakening men physically and mentally. 'And on the corpses of some of the dead small spots were visible, not unlike those which we see to blotch the skin of plague victims.'

Despite the fact that Bigges and others would have known what plague symptoms looked like, this sounds more like scarlet fever than bubonic plague, if only because of the relatively low mortality rate. This made the fleet a far less formidable force than it may have been. The journey was slow and tiring. They put in to St Christopher's (St Kitts) to 'refresh our sick and clean and air our ships,' as Bigges wrote.

A month behind schedule, Drake abandoned attacking Marguerita, and after a council of war with his captains, pressed on to one of his main targets, Santo Domingo in Hispaniola, a big centre for the slave trade since 1501. A frigate headed the same way was persuaded to guide the fleet into the harbour, with the warning that the place was heavily defended and difficult to attack. The troops were placed in the pinnaces and boats, Carleill at the bow of the barque *Francis*.

On New Year's Day 1587, the force landed on a broad sandy shore 9 miles west of 'the most elegant' city of Santo Domingo. The land troops, musketeers protected by pikemen, marched to the city gates and opened fire on the militia drawn up against them. Carleill had divided his force and attacked the sea and landward gates simultaneously, hacking his way through to the market square, which was the most easily defended part of the city.

The next day, the units moved out from this hub, taking strong points and street corners and protecting them with trenches and guns. No doubt Bigges' account reads a little too smoothly, but it seems to have been a master class in urban warfare. Burning the city was hell, however, the temperatures after 9 in the morning already unbearable. Drake insisted that the ransom price for the rest of Santo Domingo was a minimum of 25,000 pieces of gold.

Both Drake and Frobisher would have been amused, if they saw it, by the huge piece of cast-iron artwork in the governor's palace. Philip of Spain sat on a rearing horse, its hind hooves on a globe and emerging from the King's mouth, the motto '*Non Sufficit Orbis*' – 'the world is not enough'. In their respective ways, both men were doing their bit to make sure that Philip had less of the world, day by day and town by town.

As well as the ransom, Drake gained three vessels in his fleet. An officer aboard the *Primrose* wrote: 'Thus the Spaniards gave us the town for a New Year's gift.'[3] The gift was not as great as hoped, however, for in negotiating the town's ransom, despite threats of its total destruction, Drake was after all only able to negotiate 25,000 ducats as opposed to the ½ million for which he had hoped. Once again, even in a city as opulent as Santo Domingo, the silver plate was negligible, the gold virtually non-existent. Bigges wrote of the sugar, ginger, cattle hides, wine, oil, vinegar, silk cloth and 'elegantly glazed clay (which they call porcelain, transported there from the East Indies)' and glass, but it was not the fortune Drake had promised the Queen.

The fleet pressed on to the next potential gold mine of Cartagena. The governor, Pedro Fernandez de Busho, had heard of Drake's previous victories and, although shaken, had begun to make preparations. The city was already defended by a fort and two large galleys. He augmented this with trenches dug around the town's perimeter mounted with guns. The beach and isthmus leading to the city wall bristled with sharpened spikes, placed there by the 200 Indians who were part of a 700-strong force. Even the clergy were armed. Hearing of Drake's use of inland attack, the governor deployed troops to defend the town bridge, the sole access point, re-garrisoned the fort and sent men beyond it into the anchorage of the lagoon below. The English fleet were surprised by the extent of the defences and some were openly doubtful. Again, the officer of the *Primrose* wrote: 'It is impossible by man's reason for us to win. [It is not] likely that any man of us should escape.'[4]

Drake carried out some reconnaissance, capturing two local fishermen who told him of the beach covered with sharpened spikes. Landing a significant force on that side of the bay, Carleill advanced. Knowing of the trap that had been laid for them, they marched below the waterline, scattering the small Spanish force before them. Bigges (or Croftes if Bigges was killed in this encounter) wrote: 'Our pikes were larger than theirs, our bodies better armoured so that they could not adequately withstand the blows of our weapons.' The Indians with the Cartagena force used poisoned arrows and blow darts, almost certainly the first time English troops had been exposed to them. They also planted the darts like caltraps, barbs uppermost, to catch the feet of the unwary.

Indicative of Drake putting his favourite in the path of glory, he sent Frobisher into the far more dangerous waters with the fleet's pinnaces to try to attack the fort. 'The main mast beaten to pieces, the oars stricken out of our men's hands . . . and our captain like to have been slain'.

Drake's command stayed at Cartagena for six weeks whilst the wounded recovered, but the fever stayed with them too. The Spaniards referred to this as *calenture*, a hot fever, causing delirium. Many of the men came to believe that the 'unclean night air which they call *la serena*' was responsible – only the natives were immune to it. It was this sickness, Bigges or his continuator contend, that prevented Drake and Frobisher from sailing on to Nombre de Dios and making the overland crossing to Panama.

Again, the financial recompense was small. Even though Drake burnt a quarter of Cartagena in an attempt to raise more money, he only received £110,000, with an additional £10,000 for not burning a Franciscan friary and returning some high-profile hostages. By now dissention amongst the crew had turned to resignation. Limping back up the coast they in turns treated the locals civilly with lavish feasts and then burned their buildings – the bewildering paranoia of conquerors throughout time. The booty ship, called the *New Year's Gift* after Santo Domingo, sprang a leak and had to be shadowed by the *Talbot* in case she sank. They aborted attempts to attack Havana, which had been preparing for the arrival of Drakes' fleet for months, building extra defences and drilling men. The fleet was running dangerously low on fresh water – 'the best mistress of things,' as Croftes wrote – and eventually put in on the coast of Florida.

They came upon the port of San Juan on the St Augustine River purely by accident and were able to walk in unchallenged having shot the fort's ensign from its tower. Much of the Bigges/Croftes account, written by soldiers, inevitably refers to land engagements, perhaps because they were unaware of what the fleet was doing offshore to protect them. At San Juan, however, the vice-admiral (Frobisher) travelled upriver in a pinnace and was fired on from the fort's ramparts before the defenders fled. The most serious loss to the English occurred now when Sergeant-Major Anthony Powell (a Brigadier in twenty-first-century terminology) was shot through the head in an ambush. There they found £6,000, small recompense for a crippled fleet. That stretch of the Florida/Virginia coast was unknown to anyone in the expedition and soundings taken by Drake and Frobisher registered a depth of a mere 3½ fathoms.

On 9 June, the fleet sighted a huge fire near the shore and Carleill sent a skiff to investigate. The locals were Englishmen – this was Walter Ralegh's colony of Roanoke. In harbour here the next day, a serious storm arose and forced the fleet to scatter, some heading home, whilst others – the *Francis* and two pinnaces – rode it out and stayed put. When they set sail days later, a number of the demoralized and depressed 'Virginians' came home with them. The return home in fact fell somewhere between the glory of Drake in 1580 and the disaster of Frobisher in 1578.

The main fleet sighted land on the 25th and put into Portsmouth the following day, 'all of us,' as Croftes wrote cheerily, 'hale and hearty'. He remained positive in his summation of what the expedition had achieved – £60,000 in cash and 240 cannon for the loss of 750 men, including at least 15 captains, amongst them Carleill's own nephew Alexander.

What Drake and Frobisher had done was to dent Spain's pride and to humiliate her colonial governors. Philip was obliged to send ships and men to protect those far flung outposts of empire at a time when he needed them for the 'enterprise of England' and to defeat the rebellious Dutch.

But that was not how Elizabeth and her government viewed matters. Drake appears to us not as the faultless hero of legend. His men must have realized, as Frobisher's had seven years earlier, that he was not a great explorer. Bombast and symbolism gave way to truth and failure.

Chapter 9

Armada

Tensions between increasingly Protestant England and the Catholic super-power of the day, Spain, had been growing throughout Martin Frobisher's adult life. When Walsingham's spies uncovered the Throckmorton Plot in 1583, Francis Throckmorton's confessions, albeit under torture, implicated Bernadino de Mendoza, Philip II's ambassador in London. He was ordered to leave England and the whole business stood as a significant nail in the coffin of Anglo-Spanish relations.

At the Queen's court, her on–off lover, the Earl of Leicester and Walsingham himself represented a patriotic Protestant pressure group which constantly urged on Elizabeth a more aggressive foreign policy and wholeheartedly promoted the kind of piracy in which Drake and Frobisher had participated in the West Indies. It was only the more-cautious Burghley who kept this group in check.

In Philip's palace of the Escorial, there were similar pressures placed on the King. Painted by Dutch Protestants in particular as a fanatic despot, he was actually as reluctant as Elizabeth to go to war and, like her, he was constantly vacillating in the early 1580s against the pressure of Admiral Santa Cruz, who was itching to unleash his fleet against England.

By 1585 it looked as though Philip might be able to control the weak French government of Henri III and if this were the case, not only would the French Huguenots be forced into conversion by the sword, but Spain would dominate all

Europe, holding territory on the Western seaboard from the Frisian Islands to Gibraltar. Faced with this situation, Elizabeth agreed under the Treaty of Nonsuch in August to send 5,000 Foot and 1,000 Horse under the control of the Earl of Leicester, to support the Dutch rebels. In the event, Leicester proved the wrong man for the job. He arrogantly took on himself the title of governor-general, allied himself with the extreme Protestant Calvinist group and ran up huge bills for almost no military return.

The discovery of the Babington Plot by Walsingham in July 1586 triggered what was to become 'the enterprise of England'. Anthony Babington was yet another disillusioned Catholic working to ensure the release of Mary, Queen of Scots, from her position under house arrest. Letters flying secretly between them and Mendoza, now Spanish ambassador in Paris, were intercepted by Walsingham's agents and proved conclusively that Mary intended to lead an armed insurrection against her cousin. This was obvious treason and Mary was found guilty in October and sentenced to death. For four months Elizabeth agonized over this, against united pressure from the whole of her Privy Council. In the end, she agreed, spending days in her infamous rages and Mary's shaved head rolled across the floor at Fotheringhay Castle on 18 February 1587.

Still Philip dithered, but he could not deny the accusations levelled by his chief minister, Juan de Idiaquez, that England was 'at present stirring up the Netherlands, troubling the Indies and infesting the ocean'[1] The execution of Mary, however, tipped the balance. The Babington letters had contained news that Mary had declared Philip, not her young son James, as her heir and with her gone, Philip could now pose as a man rightly safeguarding his inheritance and seeking revenge against a deeply offensive act – regicide. Because of this, he also found a reluctant ally in the new, previously anti-Spanish Pope, Sixtus V.

The 'enterprise of England' was delayed for a year. Such an invasion was expensive and required a vast amount of organization. Santa Cruz, charged with all this, spent almost 4 million ducats fitting out a grand fleet of 500 ships, which would carry 60,000 troops to the south coast of England. Ship to ship at sea, the contrast between Spanish and English fleets would hang in the balance, but once on dry land, the hard–bitten veterans of Alexander Farnese, the Duke of Parma, would walk all over the half–trained militiamen of Elizabeth's England.

What really delayed the invasion was the famous 'singeing of the king of Spain's beard' by Francis Drake. In April 1587, Drake attacked Cadiz, the principal Spanish port, and sending in his deadly fire–ships, destroyed twenty–four galleons of the line before continuing to Cape St Vincent to destroy vital provisions being collected for the fleet. The death of Santa Cruz in February 1588 delayed things still further and his chosen successor, the Duke of Medina Sidonia, was essentially a pen–pusher, not a warrior. By May, however, all was ready and the greatest Armada Europe had ever seen was sailing north to liaise with Parma's troops in the Netherlands.

How ready was the English Navy for what was facing them? Its commander, Lord Howard of Effingham, had eighteen galleons at his disposal, the lightest at 300 tons, and a century of shipbuilding and innovation had created a fighting unit capable of outgunning and outmanoeuvring anything that Spain could muster. There were seven smaller galleons, usually called ships, that weighed a 100 tons or more, and the pinnaces, which were 'the eyes and ears' of the fleet, light, fast and used for reconnaissance, the sending of dispatches and any work necessary in shallow waters or near the coast. We have seen them in action already, both for exploration and war.

The galleons usually had two decks and cannon arranged to fire broadsides when two ships exchanged fire alongside each other. At the bows and stern were castles – fo'csle and aftcastle – which were platforms and the legacy of medieval naval warfare. Here stood lighter cannon or men with matchlocks.

The heaviest of the armed merchantmen, the greatships, carried heavy cannon called culverins and were so like the conventional galleon that they were often mistaken for warships. Other vessels that had a double usage were caravels and hoys, crumsters and galliots and several of these would probably have been drummed into service by both sides in the duel that followed.

The guns had several names depending on category and weight. In the English Navy, a cannon had an 8in calibre, a 12ft barrel and fired the heaviest shot available – 64lb of iron. These guns weighed 7,500lb and were made of iron or brass. Demi-cannon, culverin, demi-culverin, saker, minion and falcon were smaller artillery pieces. The smallest, the falconet, had a 2¼in calibre, 5ft barrel, firing cannon balls of 1½lb. These guns, mounted on the 'castles', weighed between 360 and 400lb. Since the guns' range was not much more than 500yd to be effective, close-quarter fighting was essential. A 'long culverin shot' could be as much as 2 miles, but everything depended on the condition of the guns, the speed of the gunners, the state of the sea and the direction of the wind. There seems to have been little consistency in the 1580s in terms of gunnery and some ships' companies were better than others. Shortly before the *Mary Rose* sank off Spithead in 1545, her commander complained to a passing captain that he had 'the sort of knaves he could not rule'.

The work of John Hawkins as treasurer of the Navy since 1578 had seen the transformation of English galleons so that the castles were lowered and the hulls more streamlined. These were the race-built ships that were to revolutionize naval warfare. Older captains, including Martin Frobisher, were probably unhappy with this tinkering. The 'majesty and terror' of high castles gave the galleons of Spain a colossal psychological advantage before they even fired a shot. Under the imaginative work of William Wynter, the Navy's armaments had undergone a transformation too. Cannon were now largely of brass, not iron, firing 18 or 9lb shot at ranges of over 1,000yd. It is uncertain how many of the Queen's ships were armed in this way by 1588, but an inventory compiled three years earlier shows that twenty-one of them had the new light port pieces, fowlers and bases, the last two of which were swivel guns.

Against all this, Philip's mighty Armada, sailing when possible in a crescent formation, numbered 130 ships; 20 huge galleons from the Castilian and Portuguese squadrons and 4 from New Spain. Making up a sort of reserve were 41 merchantmen, together with pinnaces and supply ships. The whole carried 2,431 guns and 22,000 sailors and soldiers.

Ironically, we know a great deal more about the Armada than the English fleet opposing it. Medina Sidonia was a stickler for paperwork and each ship was listed with its squadron in the battle order, together with each ship's companies, medical facilities, preaching friars, gunners, gentlemen–adventurers and so on. Provisions (hastily reassembled after the Cadiz raid) included cheese, fish, rice, wine, oil, vinegar, biscuits, beans, bread and, of course, water. Bizarrely, this was published not once but several times, with updates and corrections. Burghley certainly had a copy, even if Howard, already at sea, did not. Undoubtedly, the purpose of all this was to overawe the enemy. How could *any* nation stand up to the might of imperial Spain?

When adverse weather conditions began to break the fleet's formation, conflicting reports reached London, Lisbon and Madrid, some suggesting that the enterprise had been abandoned until the following year. Therefore, it may have come as a surprise when Captain Thomas Fleming on the *Golden Hind* sighted a large fleet off the Scilly Isles. The story of Francis Drake playing bowls on Plymouth Hoe when Fleming's news arrived is probably apocryphal. Drake was technically vice-admiral under Howard, but the man's reputation was huge. To the Spaniards, he was El Draque, The Dragon, and they were undoubtedly afraid of him.

One man who was not was Martin Frobisher, waiting for news at Plymouth on board the *Triumph*, the largest galleon in either fleet in the action that was to follow. At 740 tons, the *Triumph* was actually lighter than the *Primrose*, but the *Primrose* played no part in the campaign against the Armada. The *Triumph* was built in 1561 and although individual details have been lost, it is known that she was refitted in the late 1590s to more or less the same specifications. She carried a total of 58 guns, 2 more than the comparably armed *Elizabeth Jonas*. Aboard her high decks, which made her look more Spanish than English, were 9 demi-cannon, 4 cannon perier, 14 culverin, 7 demi-culverin, 6 saker, 2 minion, 4 port pieces, 2 fowlers and 12 bases. The crew numbered 340 sailors, 40 gunners and 120 soldiers. In the right hands – and Frobisher's *were* the right hands – she could blow any Spanish ship out of the water at considerable range.

Howard called a council of war at which Drake, Frobisher and Hawkins were given their respective commands. Along with the others, the *Triumph* slipped out of Plymouth Sound under cover of darkness, looking for the enemy.

As the enemy formation was sighted, with the Levant ships and galleasses at their head, the beacons built all along the south coast roared and crackled into light and by that means men as far away as Frobisher's Yorkshire knew that the invasion was imminent. The first shots were fired later that day as *La Rata*'s guns opened up on a nosy English pinnace that got too near. No damage was done. The lines of battle were drawn, the Armada, all black spars and towers off Dodman Point; Howard, Drake and Frobisher beyond the Eddystone Light.

The next morning, despite the fact that the weather-gauge (advantage of the wind and sea) lay with the Spaniards, Howard managed to get himself between them and the land. At this point the wind changed in the English fleet's favour and stayed that way for the next nine days. Now Medina Sidonia could see at first hand and at close quarters how much more manoeuvrable were the English ships than his. The commander ordered the crescent formation and with frightening efficiency it was created with ships making or hauling sail to adjust like troops on a parade ground. It was a formation the Turks had used at Lepanto in 1571 and it was defensively very strong; the English had seen nothing like it.

As was the tradition, whilst Frobisher in the *Triumph* took his position in the English line, Howard and Medina Sidonia exchanged challenges and the English made for the Levant squadron in the wing commanded by Alonso de Leiva. Whilst Howard's *Ark Royal* went after de Leiva's *Rata Coronada*, Frobisher, Drake and Hawkins in the *Triumph*, *Revenge* and *Victory*, hit the other wing under the command of vice-admiral Juan de Recalde.

The admiral's flagship had originally been a privately built man-of-war owned by Walter Ralegh and bearing his name (the *Ark Ralegh*). She had been built to a design by John Hawkins at Deptford and carried a massive fire-power in relation to her size. She weighed 550 tons, had a keel length of 100ft, a beam of 37ft and carried 268 sailors, 32 gunners and 100 soldiers.

The *Revenge* had also been built at Deptford and was 11 years old. She weighed 460 tons, but her exact specifications are unknown. In many ways, she is probably the most famous of the Elizabethan warships, painted green and white in the Queen's favourite colours and costing £4,000 to build. As Drake's flagship, she came through much of the fiercest fighting off the south coast and ended her days defiantly under Richard Grenville off the Azores in 1591, sinking when a storm finally destroyed her weakened hull, riddled with shot after a 16-hour firefight with a Spanish fleet.

The *Victory*, whose name was to belong to a much more famous ship later in history, was originally the *Great Christopher*, an 800-ton armed merchantman built by the City of London merchants in 1560. She carried 42 guns and had been thoroughly rebuilt two years before the Armada.

The Spanish vice-admiral's actions that summer's day do not make much sense. Alone in his flagship *San Juan de Portugal*, he turned to take on the English galleons. He was of course heavily outnumbered, but what he was probably trying to do was to force a boarding situation, in which his seasoned soldiers could grapple with the nearest ship, swing across with their ropes and irons and take a prize. The largest and most mouth-watering prize was Frobisher's and to smash the *Triumph* with his close-range guns would be an achievement. But the English galleons held off at some 300yd and pounded the *San Juan* with their longer range guns. After an hour of this, other ships came to her rescue and the English pulled away. The first day's fighting was over.

The feisty Frobisher must have been furious. He had come within range of a large capital ship and he would no doubt have loved to have taken or sunk her. He knew, as did all the captains, that the Armada was essentially unbloodied. He could not have known, in fact, that the *San Juan* had minimal damage and only a handful of crew killed and wounded. Howard's council of war that night urged caution the next day and the need to wait for reinforcements out of Plymouth. They believed, with some logic, that the Armada intended to put in to a port somewhere on the south coast. Howard had taken a risk. He was not an experienced sailor but relied on men like Frobisher to give him their words of wisdom. The problem was that there had never been a naval confrontation on this scale; there was no blueprint, no rules.

The final decision was to trail the Armada rather than trying to stop it head on, to inflict as much damage as possible and at all costs to prevent it linking up with Parma at Dunkirk or Nieweport. Drake was given the honour of leading the pursuit, the rest sailing in his wake.

Whether because of poor visibility or the speed of the *Revenge*, Howard's *Ark* got lost in the darkness and by dawn, together with the 600-ton *Mary Rose* and the 730-ton *White Bear*, had actually sailed into the Armada's formation, following the stern lights of a Spanish galleon! The official accounts of both sides are vague on this, but clearly Howard realized his situation and got out of there without a shot being fired. The Armada certainly saw them, but did not open fire or even break formation to give chase.

Drake had in fact veered off during the night in pursuit of what he believed to be the enemy and which turned out to be, according to the Devon man, German merchantmen. As dawn rose, he found the drifting flagship, the *Rosario*, of Pedro de Valdes, which had been seriously damaged in a manoeuvring accident and effectively abandoned by the rest of the Armada. Drake took the man prisoner and towed the ship into Torbay. Frobisher was furious. He and Drake had clearly been 'off hooks' since the West Indies expedition and Frobisher believed the *Rosario*'s spoils should have been more fairly distributed. This protracted battle was, after all, a joint national enterprise, not the usual privateering free-for-all to which both men were used. It could, of course, be that Frobisher was annoyed because, yet again, Drake had been in the right place at the right time to take what turned out to be the richest prize of the whole campaign; it had 46 guns and 55,000 ducats aboard. Three weeks later, Frobisher was still muttering about this, demanding that Drake share the prize money or 'I will make him spend the best blood in his belly.'

That day, two battles erupted, one off Lyme Bay as Howard tried to outmanoeuvre the Spanish fleet and got himself too close for comfort and another off Portland Bill. Frobisher's *Triumph* was at anchor here, with five merchantmen from the port of London protecting the huge ship and being attacked by four Spanish galleasses. Either Frobisher could not follow the Lord Admiral's constant change of tack (the *Triumph*, remember, was the largest ship in the entire campaign), which seems unlikely given Frobisher's seamanship and experience, or he positioned himself where he did, apparently helpless at anchor, knowing that the Shambles sandbank and the fast-running race alongside would either see an attacking ship run aground or drive her hopelessly off course. Frobisher was right if that was his plan. Hugo de Moncada's galleasses had achieved nothing after an hour, except to stand off out of range of the *Triumph*'s guns. After another hour, Howard came to Frobisher's rescue, although clearly that was unnecessary as the *Triumph* was without doubt more than holding her own.

Medina Sidonia was about to lead his sixteen-ship squadron into this melee when he realized that his own vice-admiral was in danger of being cut off and went to his aid instead. The *San Martin* blazed away against each of Howard's line that passed it and stayed afloat until both sides stopped firing.

On board the *Triumph*, as the galleasses withdrew, damage must have been minimal. No doubt timbers were splintered and canvas torn, but the body and wound count was probably slight. Throughout the day, Frobisher would have been on his poop deck, roaring orders above the cannon fire and shaking his sword at the Spaniards, who did not dare get too close to him. Even so, despite two prizes taken, it had been another frustrating day. The Armada, maintaining its crescent formation, was still sailing east on its intended course. And the English had used up almost all their ammunition.

The next day saw the heaviest casualties, when the *Gran Griffin*, heavy and sluggish, became separated from the Spanish fleet and was attacked by Drake on the seaward wing. Even so, it was still possible for the stricken ship to be towed away to relative safety. By the time Howard's fleet reached the Needles, boatloads of volunteers were sailing out to provide powder and shot, water, bread and cheese.

Howard called another war council. Frobisher's heroic stand off Portland Bill was praised, but the truth was that the English battle line could be broken, whereas it seemed the Spanish could not. It was decided to split the command into four, about twenty-five ships each, one led by Howard, one by Drake, one by Hawkins and one by Frobisher.

The calm on the next day caused difficulties, John Hawkins's *Victory* having to be towed by rowing boats into a position to attack the two Spanish stragglers that presented themselves. Medina Sidonia sent his galleasses to attack him and these in turn were fired upon by Howard to Hawkins's rear. In his official report the Lord Admiral claimed that so much damage was done to the galleasses that they were not used again, but this is simply untrue. All four of them continued up the Channel with whatever repairs were required carried out as they went.

Watchers from the beaches of the Isle of Wight must have been astonished to see, at a distance of less than 3 miles, three squadrons, including Frobisher's, closing in on the Armada. There are some grounds for believing that the Spaniards intended to put in to the island and perhaps take it, although a similar attempt by the French in 1545 had been beaten back with heavy casualties. In the event, of course, in 1588 the English fleet was in the way. Frobisher's squadron was nearest to the land and the rising wind and fast-flowing currents of St Catherine's Race drove him beyond the wing of the Spanish crescent off Dunnose Point. The *Triumph* took on the *San Martin*, Frobisher bellowing commands at his gunners, who, black-faced with powder and toiling at their places, hauled away on hemp and rammed cannonballs home.

As other galleons came to the *San Martin*'s aid, Frobisher's *Triumph* was cut off from the rest of his squadron and the vice-admiral gave desperate orders for his crewmen to lower the boats and row to safety. Other ships joined him until eleven boats were roped to the *Triumph* and rowing madly out of firing range. Suddenly, the wind changed direction and the *Triumph* was back in action, leaving Medina Sidonia to break off that attack and turn to face Drake on the other wing of the crescent.

That Thursday made Howard realize that there would be no Spanish landing on the south coast and the next day, in a morale-boosting exercise, he knighted John Hawkins and Martin Frobisher on the deck of the *Ark Royal*. At last the vice-admiral had the focus of attention he believed he had deserved for years. Merited though these accolades were, the enterprise of England was still under full sail. How can we account for this? Bearing in mind the astonishing speed and accuracy of naval gunnery in Nelson's day, two centuries later, it seems churlish, but probably accurate, to point out that it was not good in Frobisher's time. William Thomas believed that the country's sins were to blame, 'that [there was] so much powder and shot spent and so long time in fight, and in comparison thereof, so little harm?'[2]

At Whitsand Bay, the Spaniards anchored to take stock of their situation. That gave Lord Henry Seymour time to bring his squadron, blockading the Channel to prevent Parma trying to break out on his own, to support Howard. There was another council of war. Medina Sidonia at this point could have been in touch with the governor of Calais, only 30 miles away. He may already have contacted Parma away to the north. The decision was made to break up the Armada using fire-ships and Frobisher, like the other captains, went back to his squadron to organize this, stripping the ships of all stores except powder and shot, designed to explode hopefully in the heart of the Armada itself. To make matters worse for the Spaniards, the rumour spread that the Italian military architect Frederigo Gianibelli was with the English fleet, using his deadly 'hellburner' machines as floating bombs. It was not true, but the line of conventional fire-ships, at night and in tight formation, was hell enough.

Medina Sidonia fired his signal gun as usual, the command he used to call the fleet to attention, but nobody was in the mood to listen. The captains seemed to have collectively panicked and the ships scattered, only the Portuguese galleons holding their formation by moving. By contrast, the English fleet of course was intact and with Seymour's reinforcements probably numbered 150 ships, the last time the entire naval strength of the country would be gathered in one place.

Whilst Drake made for Medina Sidonia's galleons, Howard drove the last of the galleasses onto the sandbanks of Calais and in the hand-to-hand fighting from the *Ark*'s boats, Hugo de Moncada was killed and his exhausted sailors and galley-slaves swam for the safety of the shore. By the time Howard's squadron returned to the main fleet, Drake's *Revenge* was in a firefight with the *San Martin*. Suddenly he broke off, sailing north–east and taking his squadron with him. Signal guns and trumpets were used to convey orders ship to ship, but more complex manoeuvres could not easily be explained, except by messengers in a rowing boat. Drake sent nobody and Frobisher's take on the incident was born of his dislike for the man: 'He [Drake] came bragging up at the first indeed and gave them his prow [guns] and his broadside; and then kept his luff and was glad that he was gone again like a cowardly knave or traitor – I rest doubtful, but the one I will swear.'

Drake's departure brought Frobisher's squadron head to head with the *San Martin*, the *Triumph* bigger and higher in the water than the Spanish flagship and Frobisher opened up at devastating range with his great guns. Other Spanish galleons joined the melee by the time Hawkins's squadron arrived and once again reformed their defensive crescent. This was the last fight of the Armada, off Gravelines, and the slaughter was terrible. At last, the English guns were punching holes in the hulls of the galleons of Spain and for some 12 hours the battle raged. When a sudden squall blew up, with rain driving into English faces, the Spaniards were able to limp away, sails tattered, ammunition all but gone and decks awash with blood. But they still reformed into the crescent and the chase began again.

By the end of that day, it looked as if the rising seas and strong winds would destroy the Armada and Frobisher looked on as the crippled galleons were being blown towards the treacherous sandbanks off Zeeland. From the Spanish point of view, something of a miracle happened – exactly like the one that had occurred at Lepanto seventeen years earlier; the wind changed completely. This allowed the Armada to sail for deep water again and they were free. The English could not believe it, but their pursuit now was in a way pointless; they only had ammunition for about an hour's fighting.

Howard called a council of war on the *Ark*. Seymour would return to blockading duties to keep Parma on land. Everybody else would continue the pursuit since it was still possible that the Spaniards would land in the north – perhaps on Frobisher's Yorkshire coast – or in Scotland.

By the time the Queen made her famous speech to the waiting troops at Tilbury on 18 August, it was, in fact, all over. A modern historian paints a stark picture of the moment: 'a battered, rather scraggy spinster in her middle fifties perched on a fat, white horse, her teeth black, her red wig slightly askew, dangling a toy sword and wearing an absurd little piece of parade armour'.[3] However, he concedes that was not how patriotic Londoners saw it. This was Gloriana and she would lead them against the Popish armies of Spain's evil empire come what may.

Storms on that day had scattered the English fleet so that several ships took refuge in the Thames Estuary, not far from Elizabeth. Rumours flew in England and even more absurd ones in Europe: twenty-five English ships had been sunk; Drake had a leg blown off; Drake was captured. English Catholics were poised to kill the bastard queen and hand the country over to Parma, who was surely on his way. Most of the nonsensical pamphlets printed in late August focus on Drake, so that Frobisher has remained something of a footnote, even in modern historians' accounts of the campaign. Spain began to believe these stories and everywhere preparations began for huge celebrations. But slowly, the reality dawned – the great Armada was scattered who knew where in the North Sea. When Bernardino de Mendoza's delighted letter, apparently confirming a brilliant Spanish victory, reached Philip at the Escorial, the King wrote in the margin, 'Nothing of this is true. It will be well to tell him so.'

Between the end of August and the middle of October, storms battered and pounded the Armada. Ships were driven onto the Irish coast or the dangerous rocks of the Western Isles. Exhausted sailors and soldiers, lost and without food, were usually clubbed to death on the beach or hanged by order of the local authority. In some lucky cases, these survivors were sheltered by the Irish on the grounds of common religion and humanity. One of the most brilliant aspects of the entire campaign, from the Spanish viewpoint, was the fact that Medina Sidonia brought forty-four of his sixty-eight ships back to Spain. As J.H. Elliot writes: 'In terms of fighting power . . . the defeat of the Armada represented a serious, but not an overwhelming, blow to Spain.'[4] Spanish morale took a severe hit and with hindsight it can be seen that the Armada was the beginning of Spain's long and miserable decline, but in the 1590s, Spanish seapower was just as formidable as in the years before the Armada sailed.

The English fleet waited in various ports – Dover, Margate, Harwich – in case the Armada could somehow reform or Parma cross the Channel some other way. Some historians have accused Elizabeth of callousness towards her own sailors. They had won her – with a lot of help from the weather – a splendid victory and saved her country from invasion. Now they were dying of typhus in the holds of their ships, without gratitude, without pay. She had promised her men at Tilbury that great rewards would come their way. There was no sign of that now. When the captains demanded payment for their services and for their men's, there was prevarication or plain silence. In that fraught situation, Frobisher quarrelled with Drake 'in his shirt' and offered to fight him. Comrades and heroes in war had turned into petulant schoolboys in peace.

Chapter 10

Frobisher's Legacy

It is too easy to see the defeat of the Spanish Armada as the end of an era. At first sight, it appeared to be the largest possible nail in the coffin of Spanish imperialism and even to herald the arrival of the English as the greatest imperial power of any age. Neither of these hypotheses is true. The decline of Spain was highly complicated, and at its heart were economic and social, rather than military, causes. And there is far more to the rise of the English than one naval battle.

English propaganda, of course, was working overtime. The legend inscribed on one of Elizabeth's Armada medals reads 'God blew his winds and they were scattered'. The Queen had one of the most flattering portraits painted of herself – the Armada portrait – with, through the window behind her, a view of her fleet sailing proudly with all sails set and her right hand resting on a globe.

One of the men who had crossed sizeable portions of that globe was now Sir Martin Frobisher, a Queen's admiral and a hero of the Armada. The Spanish fleet might have been scattered by the 'Protestant wind', but Parma might still invade and Philip II showed no inclination to end the war. Along with the fleet commanders, Frobisher paid for wine and arrowroot to ease the comfort of their scurvy and typhoid-ridden men, as clearly the Privy Council were not going to oblige. We need not see him as too much of a hero in this; it is highly likely he and others were still pocketing monies due to their troops, for which Frobisher had been imprisoned once before.

Throughout September, October and November there were celebrations. Bells rang, medals were struck and thanks were given to God. The royal procession held in London on 26 November was the most lavish seen since the Queen's coronation. The banners of the *Rosario* hung in the nave of St Paul's and Elizabeth dined by torchlight at Somerset House along the Thames.

More sober men had to remain watchful. Frobisher, for the rest of 1588 and well into the following year, rotated command of the Channel fleet with Lord Henry Seymour (who must have been heartily sick of the Channel by this time) and Sir Henry Palmer. Palmer had fought under Leicester in the Netherlands and against the Armada, captained the *Antelope*, a 300-tonner in Seymour's blockading squadron, doing particularly stalwart work with the fire-ships off Gravelines.

In April 1589 a particularly ill-advised expedition set sail under Francis Drake with Sir John Norreys as land commander to install Don Antonio, the Prior of Crato, on the Portuguese throne, taking the war, as it were, to the enemy. Once again, Frobisher may have seethed about this, with Drake the golden boy sailing to new glory whilst he patrolled the Channel. Drake commanded 150 ships and sacked Corunna before landing near Lisbon, but here the attack faltered. Norreys lost his siege-train artillery, there was no popular rising (which everyone had expected) and more than usually oppressive heat combined with plague to decimate the English Army. In its own way, this defeat was as humiliating to Drake and England as the Armada had been to Spain and by September, Frobisher had warm work of his own.

It had long been recognized that the flow of Spanish silver from the mines of the New World was an economic lifeline to imperial Spain that should be cut. So rich was Philip's empire that he was already starting to repair the loss of the Armada and, accordingly, Frobisher, John Hawkins and George, Earl of Cumberland were sent on privateering raids to intercept this flow. This was the sort of dash and fire stuff that Frobisher loved, ravaging at will through the storms of Biscay and out into the Atlantic. So successful was this that the Flota of 1590 was nearly a year late arriving in Spain, because the galleons had had to waste time avoiding the English, or taking them on.

If Frobisher had enemies before he was made knight and admiral, he must have added to them now and accusations were made, probably well founded, of his attacking friendly as well as enemy ships during this campaign. He no doubt used the old excuse of not knowing from one day to the next who was friend and who was foe, but it did not work and by 1591 he was unemployed.

In his brief time at home, Frobisher remarried. The death of Isobel, his first wife, in a poor house, left him free to find another partner. Since his first marriage had been unhappy, it is unlikely that the by now 57-year-old was looking for love. Someone with land who could sit with him in his dotage was a different matter and in 1590, he found time from privateering to marry Dorothy, the widow of Paul Withypool from Ipswich. Dorothy had a grown daughter and a number of estates which, under the law of the time, became his. Glass Houghton, Wasenfield, Whitewood, Brockholes and Finningley Grange, all in Yorkshire, were manor houses he could add to Frobisher Hall at Altofts. Like Frobisher Hall, all of these estates have now disappeared. He also owned mills at Castleford and a 'town' house in Walthamstow. It is not likely that he had time to visit all of these properties.

By 1592, Frobisher was back in action again. Walter Ralegh, now a firm favourite with the Queen, had blotted his copybook by seducing Bess Throckmorton, one of Elizabeth's ladies in waiting. For that the Queen sent him to the Tower and his position in command of the Atlantic fleet was filled by Frobisher. In August, perhaps the largest prize ever taken, the Portuguese galleon *Madre de Dios*, was captured by Frobisher's captain John Burrows off the island of Flores in the Azores, where Richard Grenville's *Revenge* had sunk the previous year. The 1600 ton cargo of spices was valued at an astonishing £850,000. It probably grated with Frobisher that he had not taken the ship himself, but contrary winds had scattered the fleet and Burrows took advantage of an opportunity he could not pass up. The *Madre de Dios* case was one of those that shows just about everybody in Elizabethan England in a bad light. Burrows and his men sailed the prize into Dartmouth and refused to give her up. The Queen, who had a legal right to a share of the ship's contents, sent Sir Walter Ralegh to sort the impasse out. Since she had released him from gaol for this express purpose and he had become genuinely depressed at having displeased her, the pressure was on him to put things right. In fact, despite Ralegh's huge popularity with sailors and a rousing speech, Burrows' men were having none of it and Ralegh ended up giving the Queen her cut from his own purse.

By this time, after a brief stay at home, possibly at Altofts, Frobisher set sail once more, aboard the *Dainty*, a ship whose details are largely unknown.

By early 1594, the admiral was back in Yorkshire in what amounts to semi-retirement. He was by his own reckoning fifty-five years old, but he was actually at least fifty-nine. Most men were either dead by that time or were quite prepared to hang up their spurs and compasses and call it a day. Not so Martin Frobisher. Truculent and belligerent to the last, he commanded the fleet that took John Norreys to Brittany to mount an attack on the Franco-Spanish forces of the Catholic League.

In some ways this was an action replay of Norreys' work with Drake five years earlier, but there was no hoped-for resurrection by the locals this time. The expedition sailed from Plymouth on 27 August and landed at Paimpol. Here, Norreys' force took the land route whilst Frobisher sailed along the coast to Morlaix. The town was already under siege by royalist forces under Marshal Aumont and the arrival of an English fleet to batter them from the sea was probably too much for them. They surrendered.

A much more formidable obstacle was the fortress of El Leon, overlooking Crozon, and Frobisher made demands of the French commander to launch a full-frontal assault on the town. Timid commanders throughout this and the next century played a war of manoeuvre which has been likened to a chess game or even a courtly dance. The trick was to bully besieged towns into submission without heavy casualties or even necessarily firing a shot. This was not Frobisher's way at all and on 7 November, he personally led a contingent of English soldiers and sailors to attack Crozon's main gate.

Frobisher was hit by a pistol ball in the thigh, which must, because of the limited range of pistols, have been fired almost point-blank. It can be assumed that he was not wearing leg armour, which was considered an expensive waste of time and his leather buskins would not have saved him.

Carried back to the safety of his lines, Frobisher was held down as the field surgeon went to work. The neo-contemporary French surgeon Ambroise Paré disliked amputation of limbs, knowing the huge risk of blood loss and death through shock or infection. Most surgeons had altogether cruder ideas and no doubt Frobisher would have been held down with a leather pad in his mouth to prevent him chewing his tongue off whilst the surgeon probed for the lead ball. This he removed successfully and bandaged the leg.

In the two weeks of the campaign that followed, Brest was relieved by sea, although how effective Frobisher can have been remains in doubt. The surgeon had removed the ball, but not the powder-ingrained wadding charge that had entered the wound with it and this was causing gangrene. It may have been possible to save the leg even as the fleet sailed for home, but the infection had probably travelled too far and by the time the ships reached Plymouth, Frobisher was dead. It was 22 November.

In accordance with Elizabethan medical custom, the admiral was dissected and his entrails, lungs and heart were buried the next day in the churchyard of St Andrew's, Plymouth. On 14 December, a solemn procession of mourners, relatives, friends and the great and good of Elizabethan London wound its way to the south aisle of the Church of

St Giles, Cripplegate where the cadaver of Martin Frobisher, explorer, sailor and soldier, was finally laid to rest.

The church would see an equally famous burial eighty years later when the poet John Milton was interred there. A century after that, someone smashed open his grave, knocked out his teeth, stole a rib and tore wisps of hair from his scalp. Martin Frobisher was left unmolested.

It is one thing to leave a man's body alone, but what of his reputation? As with all of us, the world moves on. John Hawkins died two years after Frobisher, still on campaign off Panama. Francis Drake, Frobisher's old sparring partner, died of dysentery in the early hours of 29 January 1596 on the same expedition. Walter Ralegh lingered on, stumbling from failure to failure, ever the disgraced courtier, until his execution in 1618.

In terms of the on-going search for the North-West Passage, the men who knew Frobisher continued his work. In July 1583, whilst Frobisher himself had left the world of exploration, his friend and backer Humphrey Gilbert claimed Newfoundland for the Crown of England. Two years later, the explorer John Davis was the first to reach Cumberland Sound in what was later called Baffin Land.

Jacques Cartier, navigating the St Lawrence River to the south of Frobisher's route, was convinced that the river *was* the North-West Passage and he called the rapids he discovered near today's Montreal 'La Chine' (China). Between 1609 and 1611 Henry Hudson followed another river under the same belief, reaching what is today Albany, New York State, before turning back. In a second expedition, in the freezing conditions of James Bay, Hudson's crew refused to go further and set Hudson, his son and eight men, who remained loyal or were too ill with frostbite to have a say, adrift in an open boat. None of them was seen again. *Le Griffon*, looking for the Passage via the Great Lakes, disappeared in the snow and ice in 1679.

And legend, of course, plays its part. In 1775 a whaler found the English ship *Octavius* drifting off Greenland (Frobisher's

Friesland) with its entire crew frozen to death below decks. Depending on the winds and the tides, it is just possible that the *Octavius* would have been the first sailing ship from Europe to navigate the Passage. Could it still count, though, when all her crew were dead?

In the eighteenth century, with huge advances in navigational aids, Spain turned her attention to what had previously been seen as an English or at best French venture. Juan de la Bodega y Quadra made several attempts between 1775 and 1779 and a journal from his expedition fell into English hands, and Captain James Cook utilised it. One of the most famous explorers of his day, Cook hoped to gain the astonishing £20,000 prize offered by the British government to whoever could find the Passage. He came as close as anyone had, sailing west to east from the Nootka Sound, but icebergs blocked his path.

British naval officers Ross and Parry followed Frobisher's route in the 1820s and achieved what he could not. In 1851 Robert McClure received the accolade of finding the Passage proper by seeing (no ship could actually cut through the ice) Melville Island from Banks Island.

It was not until 1906 that the Passage was actually opened by ship for the first time and by then the treasures of Cathay were already being exploited more directly by the world's 'civilized' nations after the failure of the Boxer Rebellion in Peking (Beijing). Roald Amundsen walked into the post office at Eagle, Alaska, and sent a telegram home announcing his success. Frobisher must have turned in his grave.

What are we left with?

'In the name of God, Amen. The seventh daye of August in the yeere of our Lord God on thousand, five hundred, nynetyne and fowre, I, Martin Frobisher Knight, being in perfecte healthe and of good remembrance thancked be almighty god . . .' begins Frobisher's will.[1] It tells little of the man's character, but, like all such testaments, is a fascinating snapshot into the material values of a generation. He asked that his memorial service be held in the church at Altofts because he had no idea where he would be buried. Dame Dorothy, his widow, was to keep all her jewellery: 'chaines, bracelets, perles, buttons of gold and perle, aglettes and rings shee hath now in her possession'.[2] One wonders if any of this was lifted from the odd treasure ship? All her clothes and the plate at Frobisher Hall was hers too, up to the value of £200. She could have a third of his linen (tablecloths, napkins etc.), the beds and furniture and the entire contents of his Walthamstowe property. She was to have his two coaches and the greys that pulled them as well as the pick of his other horses. Dorothy also got ten milk cows, half a flock of sheep, household implements and moveables. She also inherited his debts.

Frobisher's executor was his nephew Peter, his brother John's son. The overseers of the will were Francis Boynton and Francis Vaughan, both Yorkshire gentlemen. All three of them were to have the colts of his Arabian bloodstock – 'my turke' – a full century before conventional wisdom tells us such horses were being bred in Britain.

In terms of property, the manor of Whitwood went to Peter, as did Frobisher Hall in Altofts, Finningley Grange and most of the other properties. The residue went to his other nephew, Darby, David Frobisher's son; in both cases, the legacy to be passed on to their male heirs. In the event of this not happening, the bequest would go to Francis Brackenbury, yet another nephew, the son of Frobisher's sister Jane. His old servant, 'of his good and faithfull service', William Haykes was given a year's annuity in lieu of rent at Whitwood and Mary Masterton the same in the Manor of Brockholts. His sister Jane got £10 a year in perpetuity at the feast days of our Lady and St Michael. Others who received gifts were Frobisher's sister's granddaughter Katherine Burrows, his niece Anne Frobisher and the unmarried one, Edith. Dorothy's grandchildren also benefited, so he was clearly more generous to his second family than to his first. Thomas Colwell, Anthony Lewis, Timothy Perrot and Richard Farrer witnessed the will. Unlike today, Colwell was also a beneficiary, taking possession of a horse worth £10.

It is not easy to love Martin Frobisher. He was querulous, cantankerous and awkward. Anything but a scholar, he seems to have avoided conventional education and was probably only partially literate. All the documents associated with his name – his letter to the five lost sailors, his petition to the Queen, his will – could have been and probably were written by someone else. He was a bluff northerner and called a spade a spade at a time when regional accents were strong and the world a big place. Too short-tempered and brash to be accepted at court for long, he was a man's man, never happier than when on the poop deck of a ship, crashing through foaming waters.

Frobisher the soldier is easier to evaluate than Frobisher the man. The gushing – and cringe-making – poetry that was produced in the late 1570s is typical of eulogies before and since. Thomas Churchyard wrote:

> O Frobusher, thy brute and name
> shalbe enroled in books,
> That whosoever after coms
> and on thy labour looks
> Shall muse and marvell at thyne actes
> and greatness of thy minde.[3]

Men like Churchyard were looking for patrons and at that point in his life (after the third voyage and before the ore proved worthless) Frobisher could be just such a man. Many titled, successful landowners kept poets on as a status symbol. Like Drake, Frobisher was best in command of an individual ship. His stalwart work on board the *Triumph* in the Armada campaign is proof of this. When called upon to carry out acts of individual bravery, he was second to none. As a field commander, in charge of squadrons or fleets, he was usually sound and did not make the impetuous mistakes of Drake, although that may have been due more to luck than judgement. But he was also hot-headed, short-tempered and petty in his dealings with other men, demanding the limelight and desperate for notice.

The whole thrust of sixteenth-century England was towards new men. The Tudors deliberately encouraged them because of the too well-known treachery of the old guard of the pre-1485 aristocracy. This hot-house atmosphere encouraged men – and a few women – of genius in every walk of life, but it incited rivalry and jealousy and was bitterly divisive. In this respect, Frobisher is probably no worse a culprit than Drake, Hawkins or Ralegh or any of the other self-made heroes who litter Elizabethan England. Without the suavity of poetic, well-read Ralegh and the luck of Francis Drake, Frobisher was thrown back on cruder methods, which usually involved attacking friendly as well as enemy ships and pulling his dagger on innumerable people who crossed him.

He comes across as grasping too. Minor gentry with no real fortune tended to throw up men like this and, again, the greed culture emanated from the court. The Queen herself was never happier than when her sea-dog privateers brought her loot at no expense to herself. She was not prepared to pay her sailors, ill with typhus in her ships, because it was not her way. When her brilliant spymaster Francis Walsingham died in 1590, he died in debt because he had paid for his royal mistress's security. She sent Ralegh out of an undeserved prison cell to which she had sent him to get her cut of a stolen vessel. 'Nobody's virtue was over nice' in this respect, Frobisher's debts and his 'leaning' on Michael Lok and others for backing was simply the order of the day.

What of Frobisher the explorer? Thomas Churchyard had a clear idea in 1578 of the purpose of the man's voyages in search of a new way to an old world: 'This is a true testimonie of great goodnesse intended; that our Nation is suche a Christian sorte and maner, refuseth no hazarde nor daunger, to bring Infidelles to the knowledge of the omnipotent God, yea, albeit great wealth and commoditie maie rise to us of their labours . . .'.[4] This implies that, somehow, the idea of enslaving the Inuit was

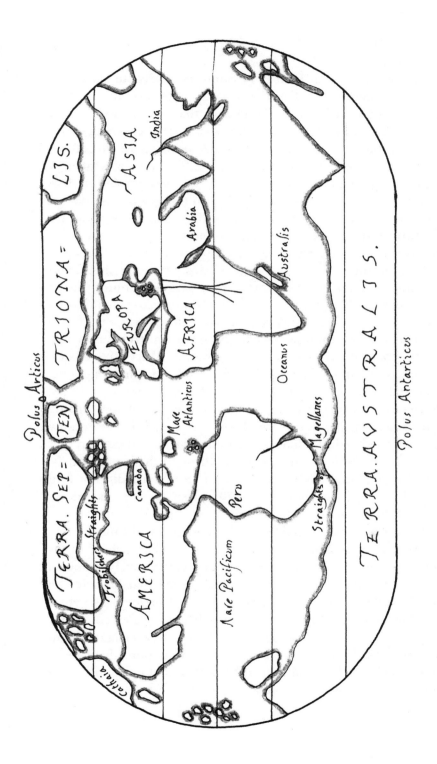

This contemporary map known as 'Frobisher's Map' optimistically shows Frobisher's Straits reaching Cathay (China) from the Atlantic. The reality was not quite like that.

acceptable because at least they would be Christian slaves. Of the Inuit themselves, Churchyard says 'these that feed like monsters (and rather live like dogges than men)'[5] and in that respect, he was merely reporting what every returning sailor from Frobisher's expeditions would have said. In today's politically correct, unreal world a very different view is taken of the native populations discovered by explorers in the past. It is understood – as it was not by the Frobishers of the world, because it never occurred to them – that each civilization has its culture, strengths and weaknesses and what is barbaric and monstrous in one, is the height of sophistication in others.

The bottom line in assessing Frobisher's contribution to exploration seems to be summed up by Thomas Churchyard in the rhetorical 'Was not this a valiant adventure, to take in hande a voyage never sailed before?'[6] This is the legacy of Martin Frobisher. The names he gave to those barren stretches of ice-encrusted land – Lok's Land, Countess of Warwick's Island, Countess of Sussex Sound, Wynter's Furnace – have all gone, superseded by later explorers like Baffin or, more recently, replaced by the original Inuktuit names they probably already had. One name has survived – Frobisher Bay. It is a testimony to a flawed expedition led by a flawed man. An expedition that so nearly succeeded. There *is* a way through the ice to Cathay. The North-West Passage is real and if Frobisher did not find it and if no one did until 1906, that is the nature of exploration.

Look up Martin Frobisher today and you will find the Bay mentioned, a handful of colleges, even an infant school in his old parish of Altofts. Someone, rather incongruously, named a rose after him. The Canadians acknowledge that he held the first Thanksgiving in North America, forty-two years before the Pilgrims. In other senses, he has been superseded. Other men – Mercator, Frisius, Hakluyt – were better navigators and geographers. Drake and Ralegh were even more devil-may-care than Frobisher. Columbus, Magellan, da Gama – they are more famous seekers of a new way to the West.

Martin Frobisher will always be the nearly man of sixteenth-century exploration, but, as Thomas Churchyard said, 'The earth was made for the children of men' and men like Martin Frobisher did their level best to take it. 'The world was not enough' for Philip of Spain and it could never be enough for Martin Frobisher either.

One thought remains. Now, at the beginning of the twenty-first century, the polar ice cap is said to be melting and that one day, quite soon, there will be an ice-free North-West Passage all year round. This may cause complications, because it will be a new permanent navigation. Canada, of course, will claim it as theirs, since it is in Canadian internal waters. But, because of the area's history, is it really Inuit, Swedish, Spanish, French and, above all, English?

Will the ghost of Martin Frobisher come back to claim his own?

Chapter 11

Our Land, Our Strength

The title of this chapter comes from the motto on the Nunavut coat of arms. Nunavut is the territory to which Baffin Island now belongs, officially established in 1993. Its capital is Iqaluit, Frobisher Bay. In 1999, the fabulous coat of arms was commissioned and designed by the elders of the region. The supporters are a caribou, standing on a rough landscape of vivid purple heather and moss, like the tundra of Baffin Island, and a narwhal on a ground of sea and ice floes. The shield bears the emblem of Nunavut (our land) and Inukshuk, a stone structure used as a territorial marker or guide post with a striking resemblance to the cairn built by Frobisher in 1576. In this new symbol, we see the esteem in which Nunavut Inuit hold their surroundings as well as their respect for the past. This was no different in the time of Frobisher. Far from being 'infidels', as Frobisher labelled them in his letter to his missing crewmen, they were a highly developed people with advanced art forms and a true knowledge of and respect for the land and for each other. With no notions of commerce, industry or expansion, the purity of their existence makes the greed and mistrust of the Europeans even less palatable.

The Thule culture arrived in the Arctic archipelago from Alaska in about 500 AD. They were, by 1000 AD, the predominant group in the region, having taken over from the Dorset culture, which had occupied the area since the second millennium BC. This was not a hostile takeover with vast armies wiping out and subjugating indigenous populations, as with the Khanate of the Golden Horde, who ravaged the comparable climatic area of Russia and Siberia to the East. Rather it was a gentle assimilation of two cultures, the traditions of which grew and developed alongside one another.

The evidence for contact before Frobisher is scant. The Norse sagas refer to 'skraelings' in the north of Vinland around Newfoundland, Labrador and Baffin Bay, although these could just as easily be interpreted as Algonquin Indians. Skraelingi in modern Icelandic means barbarian or foreigner and the derivation comes from skra meaning skins in reference to the Inuit who wore them (as opposed to the Vikings who wore woven wool). There is little in the archaeological record to indicate that Vikings had come to Baffin Bay. The most tangible evidence comes from the carbon dating of the blooms found on Kodlunarn and also smaller iron ingots found by Edward Fenton. However, there are indications that these had been exchanged between Inuit since the first millennium BC. A further clue could be the burial found by Frobisher and his men on the second voyage. There is little evidence for Inuit burial rites and a tomb of this sort may well be attributed to the Vikings, as their description of it makes it sound much like a barrow or cairn, which are typical of high-status, non-Christian and Christian burials in Europe. This is clearly open to interpretation as it refers to a skeleton found in a tomb amongst the rocks. The little evidence we do have for Dorset and Thule burials is partial skeletons placed in crevices amongst rocks. With anatomy being in its infancy, as far as laymen were concerned, it is unlikely that Frobisher and his crew would have been able to identify a full human skeleton at a glance, and, in an age of great superstition, they were unlikely to hang around this unknown grave, and offered it no Christian burial.

The Thule co-existed in small groups, moving from their semi-sedentary bases as the seasons dictated. When John Dee interviewed the Inuit brought back by Frobisher, he asked him where he came from. The answer was 'pycknea', which Dee took to be the name of the land. It sounds so like the modern Greenland 'pika', meaning 'up there', that the two men were probably looking at a map and this was Kalicho's answer. He pointed to Baffinland or the tundra and said, in effect, 'I come from up here'. In spring and summer, the Baffin Island Inuit would inhabit the coastal waters of Frobisher Bay to fish and hunt caribou. The modern Inuktituit name for the bay, Iqaluit, means place of many fish. Dionysus Settle writes of how inadequate the hide tents that made up the Inuit camps were, when in fact they were all that was required for a seasonal hunting base. The Inuit were expert fishermen using line for small fish and harpoon to hunt narwhal and whale. The Dorset culture had developed the fast and sturdy kayak somewhere around the first millennium BC and indeed these were constructed from the hides of the animals they caught and ate, as were the hooks and arrow heads made from their bone and ivory. Nothing was wasted.

As the leaves turned golden and the snow and ice of winter were ushered in, Inuit families would head north, back into the tundra, the treeless landscape so oppressive to the English, where they would live as individual families in igloos, hunting seal and polar bear. Conflict was rare between neighbouring groups. The Inuit, a term introduced in the eighteenth century for the indigenous people of Canada and Greenland, recognized the need for sharing with one another. The French used the term *esquimaux*, meaning flesh-eaters, which is used in Alaska today to include the Yupik and Inupiat groups. The spoils of the hunt were communal and even when subcultures began to develop, their names were adverts for what they had to offer to others. For example, the Inuit of West Hudson Bay were the Netsilik, or people of the place where there is seal.

Respect for the landscape is key to Inuit survival. The hunt is tied up in ritual and magic. This animistic society sees animals as equals and before the advent of the high-powered rifle the ceremony surrounding the hunt was very important.

A hunter was to get as close to his quarry as possible. This is to gain 'permission' from the animal for the hunters to take its life. If the animal fled, this was not through fear or a change in wind direction giving the hunter away, but through choice. The dogs to which the Frobisher accounts refer were huskies, which explains why Settle and others believed them to be wolves. Traditionally, the Inuit used them as pack animals, dragging sledges over the snow in tandem or fan-harness formation. They were also adept at sniffing out seal holes and even worrying polar bears as part of the hunt. To this end, soon after birth, pups have their legs pulled as part of a ritual to make them stronger and their nostrils jabbed with a bone pin to enhance their sense of smell.

The importance of animals to Inuit society is clearly displayed through their art. In contemporary Inuit culture, this has become a significant commercial element, with Inuit carvers exhibiting their work in some of the most prominent art galleries in the world. The carvings from small amulets to large soapstone sculptures reflect their belief systems and also their strong oral tradition and legend. The carvings of the Thule culture, which are small, could be considered as a form of currency. If one group had an abundance of seal in their area, a carving of a seal exchanged between groups would show this. Perhaps they would exchange it for a carving of a polar bear from higher up in the Arctic Tundra. This is perhaps supported from the development of this art after European incursion, when carvings of this sort began to depict more European things, such as figures in Victorian clothing; essentially showing what they believed the potential purchaser would like to see. These carvings also carry heavy ritual symbology; they are often marked with skeletal striations. This is tied in with the notion of the animal's soul, relating to its relationship with the natural world, with animals essentially as humans. In what was a shamanistic culture, these carvings were also used as amulets, perhaps for protection against the animals, or for luck in the hunt.

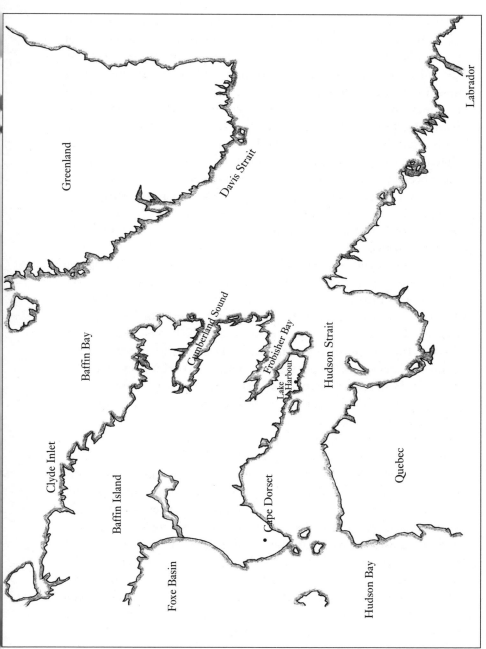

Meta Incognita today as it is today. All inlets and bays have now been explored and the area has its own airport.

There is no evidence for the Inuit having any form of two–dimensional representation. It is known that their knowledge of the landscape was vast. Maps from the period appear to us as carved bone representing the undulations of mountain ranges and form of coastlines. It is clear they understood the power of any form of pictorial representation. Snow knives, which exist from the Dorset culture onwards, are often highly decorated with legends or pictures of the hunt and it has been suggested that they may have even been used to carve out stories on the temporary canvas of the frozen tundra. As we have seen, when presented with the oil painting of his dead countryman, Kalicho became very emotional. Perhaps, as with the depictions of skeletons on Inuit carvings, he believed the soul of the man to be trapped inside the painting. Their understanding is further displayed by their skill as draughtsmen. Charles Francis Hall, whose interviews with the Inuit will be discussed shortly, was greatly impressed by their ability to draft maps and in the 1820s James Ross and W.E. Parry noted their ability to paint. Parry's British naval expedition of 1821–3 was the first to record the economic, social and religious life of the Inuit. William Parry was an evangelical Christian who served under Captain James Ross from 1818. By their return in November 1820, the pair had in fact succeeded where Frobisher had failed. The book that charted the expedition, *Journal of a Voyage to Discover a North-West Passage*, was a best-seller.

Oral tradition is very significant in Inuit culture. With no written language until the late eighteenth century, the passing of history and legend from generation to generation is very important. It helps us to understand further their belief systems and therefore their material culture, for example, the legend of the narwhal. When Kalicho and Arnaq met aboard the *Ayde*, the English seemed disappointed and bemused by their actions. Far from acting like animals and instantly becoming mates, as the English had expected, they sang to each other and talked. The two Inuit, who were unlikely ever to have known one another, as they lived over 100 miles apart on opposite sides of the bay, were probably recounting their tale of capture and, further to this, their ancestral history and legends.

During the 1860s, Charles Hall, a Cincinnati-based journalist, visited Baffin Island. He had been fascinated by the history of exploration in the Arctic since the 1850s and read much of the available literature, amassing an impressive library of books and reports of previous expeditions. He became very keen on the idea of chartering his own expedition into the Arctic with the primary aim of discovering the truth of what happened to Sir John Franklin, the British naval officer whose expedition was lost in 1845.

Franklin had been put in command of an expedition made up of two state-of-the-art vessels, HMS *Erebus* and HMS *Terror*. They were to chart and explore the North-West Passage, which had remained a fascinating and real proposition to Europeans, despite Frobisher's disappointments. Franklin had already successfully charted a vast portion of the North American coastline, and despite being 59 when he took command, he was seen as the best the Navy had to offer. He and his expedition were last seen by the *Prince of Wales*, a whaling vessel moored off Lancaster Sound in the Arctic Archipelago. Nothing more was heard of them for two years. After a third year, and much pleading from Lady Franklin, along with a large reward, many US and English vessels became involved in the search, some falling victim to the Arctic themselves. In 1850, a number of graves were found from the Franklin expedition and their fate was decided. In 1854, Dr John Rae discovered from Inuit around Boothia Bay, near to where the graves had been discovered, that the men had all died of the extremes of cold, and starvation. Most horrifically, they were said to have cannibalized each other in desperation. When news of this reached Victorian England, it was treated with horror and outrage, and none believed that a hero such as Sir John Franklin would have been capable of such atrocities. It was only in a report in 1998, on an autopsy of the bones from the burials, that cut marks on the bones, though not the reason for the men's deaths, were testament to the fact that they had indeed been cannibalized.

Hall, unfazed by what prudish Victorian society thought, realized that talking to the local populations might well be the key to finding out the truth of the Franklin expedition and, potentially, much of the history that he had read in so many European accounts. He was unable to finance his own voyage, but did gain passage on an American whaler, the *George Henry*, and set sail in 1860, stopping in Baffin Island, where he wintered.

Hall had the benefit of Inuit guides and interpreters. The Inuit had become valued additions to crews of expeditions and whaling ships. They knew the geography of the land and the nature of the climate, and they were often the reason that other European and American seafarers did not suffer the same fate as Franklin. They were also fine draftsmen and made very accurate maps for sailors. Although no Englishman made much effort to learn Inuktitut, the language of the Inuit, many Inuit learned English to be of more use to the Europeans, as they adopted elements of their material culture, such as dress and tobacco. It is important to take into account that the Inuit, by their very nature, were always willing to help their fellow man, and Europeans, who were clearly now here to stay with whaling fleets filling the waters of the Arctic and the land becoming more populous, would have been extended the same courtesy.

As Hall was wintering on Baffin Island, his guides, led by a hunter named Koojesse, had no problems in taking him to Frobisher Bay and specifically Countess of Warwick Sound in the summer of 1861. They told him of places in the landscape where there was brick and tile, timber and buildings. The Kodlunarn cairn that Frobisher had built on the second voyage had become a shrine for Inuit hunters, who placed gifts there in the hope of luck for the hunt. Fenton makes mention of finding similar structures in the landscape not attributed to the English, so possibly the Inuit already had a tradition of building such structures, and Frobisher's was merely seen as an ancestral relic. The fact that the inukshuk appears on the flag on Nunavut shows that it is a significant symbol even today. Hall was taken to Newland Island, formerly Wynter's Furnace. His guide there was an Inuit woman whom he dubbed Suzhi, she was English-speaking and knew the area well.

Hall was keen to see the artefacts in the landscape of which he had heard tell. On Newland Island, he was excited to find an aged pile of coal; it had clearly been there for some time and Hall determined it to be from Frobisher's occupation, particularly when his guide said it had been there 'a great many years'. Inuit oral tradition does not use chronology in terms of days, years or centuries, the use of 'great' and 'many' would have extended beyond even a hundred years ago. Hall's conclusions were correct if one looks at the archaeological evidence from the excavations of the 1980s and 1990s. From maps that Hall had many of his guides draw, he became the first white man to ascertain that Frobisher Bay was a bay and not a strait. That discovery had taken nearly 300 years. He subsequently visited Kodlunarn, literally 'white man's land' – the name would be enough for an intrepid historian to wish to investigate. He was told of a large metal object that had been on the island, but was no longer there. It had been variously used as a bench and a test of strength. From drawings, descriptions and even a carving, it was clear that it was an anvil. The Inuit showed him the foundation of the accompanying smithy. He recorded the length and depth of the open-cast mines on the north of the island, the Inuit referred to these as the ship trench and the other as a water (reservoir) trench. There had been a shallow well on Kodlunarn during Frobisher's time; with a lack of fresh water, it is likely to have been filled with melted snow. The identification of one of the larger trenches as a well by the Inuit perhaps suggests what their subsequent use for it was; they were known to have reused brick and tile from the site. Hall carefully recorded the foundations of the buildings, the longhouse, Fenton's House and collected charcoal, tiles and brick, along with the iron bloom he would later present to the Smithsonian.

Hall emerges as one of the first true anthropologists, as well as a keen and thorough historian. He entrusted himself totally to the Inuit, never demanding or trying to take command; he travelled with them alone. He traded tobacco for information. This could potentially lead to Inuit giving him the answers they thought he required, but the stories he was told are very compelling, and he had not given them any information from which to form a story. Where Hall really excels is in his interviews. He spoke to several Inuit from the Baffin area, including one of its oldest inhabitants, whom he named as Ookijoxy Ninoo, although his true Inuit name was probably closer to Uqitijuasi Nauk. He questioned many interviewees twice, a shrewd move, as this enabled him to identify inconsistencies in the answers and work out whether he was merely being told what he wanted to hear, which he also safeguarded against by his line of questioning, which was quite obtuse.

His interpreter for the interviews was Tookoolito, known as Hannah. Hall had met her and her husband, Ebierbing (Joe), aboard the *George Henry*. They were friends of the ship's skipper, Captain Budington. They had been in England for three years and toured the country as a living exhibition of Inuit life. They had been presented to Queen Victoria, and returned with a certain degree of English 'propriety'; Hannah wore Western dress over her insulating hide clothing. Ebierbing was actually Ipiirviq in the Inuktitut language, but the whalers of Cumberland Sound had nicknamed him Joe for obvious reasons. He and 'Hannah' were taken to Hull in 1852 by the whaler Thomas Bowlby. Always at pains to explain that Joe and Hannah were Christians and married in a Christian tradition, Bowlby exhibited the pair in native costume at a number of venues all over England.

The answers Hall received from the interviews were incredible: 'First one, then two or three, then many-very many vessels'.[1] This response should be considered first as it mirrors the numbers involved in the Frobisher voyages so closely. One of the trenches, referred to as the ship trench, was related to the repairs of vessels, which occurred particularly frequently on the third Frobisher voyage. This also appears in the interview responses – 'a big mast was raised'. He was told of the death of the Inuit at Bloody Point, and the capture of two Inuk or men. The microcosmic nature of Inuit society was a thing of the past, where Arnaq and Kalicho were unlikely to have known each other. The world was now a smaller place. Inuit migratory patterns had changed, they were now beginning to live in larger communities, and a legend of such magnitude would have spread all over Baffin Island.

He was also told of the five sailors. They had endured one winter with the Inuit, then taken a boat, perhaps the pinnace, and sailed, it is assumed, homewards. Interestingly, the Inuit tradition, which of course does not accord with Frobisher's, is that the five men effectively jumped ship because of the hardship of the expedition and had then been abandoned. This is the only time when the Inuit could have been obliged to tell the qallunaat, the Inuit name for Europeans, and now, Americans, a softer tale. Perhaps the Inuit had killed them, but the current Baffin Inuit were embarrassed by their past; perhaps the tale had altered over time for similar reasons.

What is encouraging in terms of the Inuit distorting the truth to suit their situation and that of Hall is the frequency with which they were prepared to say they did not know the answer to questions, rather than proffer any kind of response for the sake of it. Hall gives an excellent insight not only into the archaeology of the site, but also the legacy of the Frobisher voyages to the Inuit, their interpretation of its landscape and their incredible oral tradition. In 1862, Hall gave a lecture on the Frobisher relics to the American Geographical Society, with Joe, Hannah and their son, Butterfly, present. The showman P. T. Barnum was to display the blooms and other artefacts, but since he did not pay up, Hall withdrew them. The tour took its toll and Butterfly died a few weeks later.

The Inuit appear to us as one of the least aggressive indigenous people Europeans came into contact with, despite the fact that they clashed with Frobisher. It is likely, given the man's temperament, that he met trouble more than halfway and, naturally, they responded. Equally they were not put through, in later centuries, quite as much imperialist persecution as some. A look at today's map makes it clear that the Inuit still have their cherished land. The wholesale slaughter of native Americans further south between the sixteenth and nineteenth centuries shows an altogether different pattern of colonization. As the Oglala shaman Sitting Bull is reputed to have said: 'The white man broke every promise except one. He promised to take our land and he took it.'

Appendix

Frobisher's Ships

Ships of the Line

As an island, Britain relied heavily on her Navy, both the Royal branch, which operated essentially as a defensive force – what was called in Nelson's day 'the wooden walls of England' – and the Merchant fleet, which crossed the world carrying raw materials and finished goods. The Elizabethan era saw a huge expansion of all this, with new lands being discovered and settled and new raw materials being extracted from those new lands. The distinction between Royal and Merchant fleets was not clear-cut; merchantmen carried guns to protect themselves against piracy.

The state-of-the-art ship in the 1520s was the galleon, a Spanish hybrid of the earlier carrack or 'great ship' – such as the *Mary Rose* that sank off Portsmouth in 1545 – and the carvel, of which Columbus's *Santa Maria* is an example. Such ships may have been ponderous by comparison with their English equivalents by the time of the Armada, but they were faster, more manoeuvrable and stabler than anything that had gone before.

In the reign of Mary (who was married to Philip of Spain) English dockyards produced the first galleon, the *Philip and Mary*, in 1554, quickly followed by two others. Essentially then, although men like Martin Frobisher would probably never have accepted it, the Elizabethan warship was built from a Spanish prototype.

The galleons that Frobisher captained were lower in the water than the great ships and could carry more guns. The mast and sail arrangement – three masts and a combination of square and lateen-rigged sails – had not changed. The first three English galleons remained in service for over sixty years each, reflecting their efficacy and also the huge cost of shipbuilding. Where possible, old ships were refitted rather than new ones built, especially in the reign of Elizabeth, who was notoriously tight with money.

In 1558 the Royal Navy had sixteen vessels that today would be described as battleships, that is the largest, heaviest-gunned ships afloat. The largest was the *Jesus of Lubeck*, bought in Hamburg in 1544 and one of the few great ships to survive from the reign of Henry VIII. She became the flagship of John Hawkins and he seriously modified her, but she was always difficult to sail and was sunk off Vera Cruz in 1568. The *Golden Lion* was a 600-ton ship, one of the three galleons built under Mary. She carried forty guns and was not actually decommissioned until 1698, by which time she had served in three wars against the Dutch. The *Mary Rose*, renamed after the 1545 loss also displaced 600 tons and the remainder – the *Philip and Mary*, the *Hart*, the *Antelope*, the *Minion*, the *Swallow*, the *Great Bark*, the *New Bark*, the *Greyhound*, the *Jennet*, the *Mermaid*, the *Tiger*, the *Bull* and the *Mary Willoughby* – were correspondingly smaller and carried fewer guns. Alone in the list, the *Mermaid* was a French warship, taken as a 'prize' and drafted into the English fleet. Martin Frobisher's flagship in the Armada, the huge *Triumph* (740 tons), was built in 1561, the largest ship in either the English or the Spanish navies. The *Ayde*, the ship that Frobisher took on his third voyage to Meta Incognita, was far smaller at 240 tons and was built at Deptford in 1562.

The Navy also had smaller vessels – galleasses, galleys, pinnaces and barks – which were used for reconnaissance, swift darting raids and exploration. The waters around the British coast were not ideal for galleys, as cross-currents and contrary winds made life difficult for the oarsmen.

The period from 1559 to the 1620s saw England at loggerheads with Spain. It was not always a 'hot' war, but the very real threat of invasion meant that the Navy had to be on constant alert and its leaders alive to new ideas and the up-to-date technology available. From this came the race-built galleons of John Hawkins, who teamed up with master shipwright Richard Chapman in 1570. The 300-ton *Foresight* was the prototype, with a length to beam ratio of 3:1 and a stepped gun deck. The hull had a sweeping curve from stern to bows with a long beakhead and a slightly angled foremast positioned nearer the bows than usual. Her hold was 14ft deep and she carried twenty-eight guns, a lot for such a small vessel. Later examples were the *Bull*, the *Tiger*, the *Dreadnought*, the *Swiftsure* and the 100-ton lightweights *Achates* and *Handmaid*.

By the 1580s, Elizabeth's Navy was divided into three categories. First was the sort of ship used as merchantmen – the type that Frobisher took to search for the North-West Passage. They were squat, rather slow to manoeuvre and not able to keep up with the warships. They could patrol the coast, however, in search of enemy sails and with their wide, deep holds were excellent for carrying supplies. It is worth noting at this stage that no sixteenth-century ship was built to withstand the pressure of pack ice. The second category comprised the armed merchantmen – the ships that Frobisher took on his second and third voyages. The third contained the full-blown warships, virtually all of them by the time of the Armada race-built to Hawkins's specifications.

From 1577, John Hawkins was Treasurer of the Navy and no one was more adept at modifying the new ships that he himself had designed. He formed a two-tier gun-deck system, with the heavier weapons below, which added stability to the vessels, and double-clad the hulls and keels with timbers padded with hair and tar to make them longer lasting and more serviceable. The *Revenge*, the *Rainbow* and the *Vanguard* were all built to the new specifications in the 1580s, either at Deptford or Woolwich. In all, twelve of the original sixteen were converted to the race-built type and if anyone should be credited with saving England from Spanish invasion in 1588, it is John Hawkins.

Shipbuilding

The shipyards of Frobisher's time were concentrated in the south. Deptford and Woolwich were the cradles of most of Elizabeth's warships and it was not until a century later that Chatham, Plymouth, Portsmouth and Buckler's Hard went into serious production. Later still, in the era of steel and steam, the whole shipbuilding industry moved north to the Tyne and the Clyde.

The basic building materials for all ships were timber, rope and canvas. Oak and elm were the hardest English woods and there was still in the sixteenth century a plentiful supply of forests. Even so, increased trade in the Muscovy Company would see the hardwoods of Russia being used to augment the supply via the Baltic within a few years.

Matthew Baker wrote *Fragments of Ancient English Shipwrightry* in 1582 so a written record exists of how Frobisher's ships were built. There is also the archaeology of the *Mary Rose* (1545) and the anonymous merchantman known as the 'Alderney Wreck' (1592) to flesh out Baker's bones.

The ships of the time were laid down in dry docks with the keel, transom and frame laid in place using scarf joints. The planking was then fitted onto these frames in carvel style, each plank edge to edge with another. The 'ribcage' of the vessel came next, 'C' or horseshoe-shaped hoops, open at the top to take the deck timbers. Each frame was carefully measured, tapering towards bows and stern and was held in place with 'knees' and futtocks that provided extra support and rigidity.

The outer hull was made of 'ship-shaped' planks called wales and finally 'stringers', cross-braces, were placed from one side of the hull to the other. When afloat, these ships looked squat because the hulls bulged out just above the water line. Below of course, they curved in sharply to the keel. The decks themselves had a slight curve so that rainwater ran off over the ship's side.

The finest shipbuilders of the day, men whom Frobisher almost certainly knew, were Matthew Baker, Royal Master Shipwright, Robert Chapman and Peter Pett. All three men worked with Hawkins on the race-built galleons in the 1570s.

Contemporary pictures of warships in particular show them brightly painted with heraldic emblems and with flags fluttering from every spar and masthead. Figureheads were common, often gilded and almost certainly considered as the 'soul' of the ship by superstitious sailors.

Life onboard Ship
No amount of mathematical text, technical dimensions and even archaeology can give us much of a feel for what life was like for Frobisher and his men, living on one of these vessels for weeks or even months on end. The *Mary Rose*, astonishing though its finds are, is actually a huge lump of wood, only part of the keel and one side of the hull having survived. The Newport ship, a late fifteenth-century merchantman, found by chance in the recent rebuilding of the town's dock area, is actually in pieces in water tanks, like a huge construction kit awaiting assembly.

There are no hard and fast facts about the daily life of sailors in Frobisher's navy. Cut off as ships were from land, the law was interpreted by the captain and some were more notorious than others. On long dangerous voyages into the unknown, where the death rate was likely to be high, it was easy for captains to be too severe. They had to maintain discipline and the usual way was to punish harshly. Certainly on his voyages of exploration, Frobisher won few friends. It was worse for Henry Hudson, however. In 1611, searching in icy seas for the North-West Passage, his crew mutinied and cast him adrift in an open boat with his son and a handful of loyal crewmen. Their fate remains unknown.

Punishment was meted out to the laws of Oleron, according to one tradition, which was instituted by Eleanor of Aquitaine, the wife of Henry II of England. On land the most common crime was theft, but on board ship, it was probably more limited because of the relatively few possible culprits. It was punished traditionally by the thief being tarred and feathered (there were live chickens on board for meat and eggs) followed by being cudgelled through the gauntlet and dismissal. On a Frobisher voyage, of course, dismissal was hardly an option. Violence amongst the crew was carefully watched. Everyone carried a dagger in Elizabethan England but drawing one in anger on board ship could lead to the loss of a hand. Given the high risk of infection, such punishment was life threatening. In the case of murder, the killer was roped together with his victim and both were thrown overboard. In what was a godly age, whether Protestant or Catholic, a spike was driven through the tongue in cases of blasphemy.

Captains like Frobisher had to be Solomon. He had the power of life and death over his men, but for the sake of survival, especially when nature was the real enemy, even he probably turned a blind eye to some misdemeanours.

Overcrowding was a major problem. There were no hammocks on English ships until the 1590s, so the men slept on the decks wherever they could find space, often between the guns. On the North-West Passage voyages the cold precluded sleeping on the top deck, so that increased the problem.

Food and water had to be stored on board, making basic assumptions about travelling time – and of course these could be wrong. Both were restricted because sea-water was undrinkable and the food supply would eventually run out. For a voyage like Frobisher's, the *Ayde*, for example, would stock up on oxen, sheep, pigs and chickens, so the noise and smell on board would have been horrendous. On fish days – Mondays, Wednesdays and Fridays – the consumption allowed was 1lb of biscuit (very hard like modern-day dog biscuits), 1 gallon of beer, a ¼ of stockfish or ⅛ of a ling, 2oz of butter and ¼lb of cheese. Weevils infected all food so even the teeth-cracking

biscuits became soft and doughy after a while. On flesh days –
Tuesdays, Thursdays, Saturdays and Sundays – the same
amounts pertained, except that the fish was replaced by 2lb of
beef. This forms a reasonably healthy diet and every bit as good
as the labouring poor got at home. The problem was that ships'
companies were at the whim of unscrupulous pursers who
would make a profit by cutting corners in obtaining provisions.
Meat and fish was preserved in salt barrels; vegetables and eggs
in vinegar. The officers would have extras like wine, but the
famous 'grog' ration of rum had yet to be established via trade
with the West Indies. Hot food was prepared in the cook box, a
portable metal grill rather like a barbecue. Obviously great care
had to be taken because of the risk of fire in the timbers.

The risk of disease was high. A boy like John Thorne, only
12 at the time of Frobisher's third voyage, stood only a 50:50
chance of coming back. He would in theory have received 5*s* a
month, perhaps with a little more for his drumming skills, but,
again, this was at the discretion of the ship's master and all
sorts of 'necessaries' could result in the pay being docked.
Nothing was paid until the ship returned and there was no
system of pensions or of giving back-dated pay to the relatives
of a dead sailor. In the case of a privately funded voyage like
Frobisher's, the rate of pay would vary enormously. The
surgeon was well paid, but he could only set bones and stitch
wounds. Actual medicine was beyond him, although the
surgeons' instruments found on board the *Mary Rose* include
a syringe, which was probably used to inject mercury as a cure
for syphilis. The cure was worse than the disease, but at least
mercury was quicker. The biggest killer was scurvy. Months at
sea led to serious vitamin deficiencies and no one at this stage
appreciated the value of fresh fruit. At first the sufferer
became listless, then broke out in boils. His gums bled and his
teeth fell out. Before long, his painfully swollen arms and legs
refused to move. In days, he would fall into a coma followed
quickly by death.

Navigation
It is known from the various accounts of Frobisher's voyages and of the Armada that maps, charts, the compass and the cross staff were certainly used. Latitude could be worked out by the ship's pilot (in many ways the most technically qualified man on board), but longitude could only be guessed using a form of dead reckoning, based on the ship's speed and distance travelled.

Frobisher's use of maps has already been discussed here, but his pilot would also have had access to an astrolabe, an ancient Arabic instrument used in both astronomy and astrology. This consisted of a metal disc (some were wooden) with a needle called an alidade fixed to it. At noon (a visible sun was essential) the astrolabe was held up by a cord and the alidade rotated until the sun shone through the holes at either end of the astrolabe. The needle's position was then noted on marked calibrations around the edge. During the North–West Passage voyages the lack of sun for days on end limited the use of this instrument.

The cross staff was used to calculate the height of the sun above the horizon. It was made of wood, about 3ft long with a sliding crosspiece. Again, at noon the pilot held the staff vertically and operated the slide, reading the distance off the staff. It was also possible to gauge the distance from ship to shore this way.

The use of compasses on Tudor voyages and the problem of finding True North has already been discussed. Most Elizabethan ships carried four compasses; one for the helmsman, one for the pilot, one for the captain and a spare in case one of the others was lost.

The log line was a means of calculating a ship's speed. This was a length of rope attached to a triangular piece of wood that was trailed in the water around a moving ship. Knots were tied at regular intervals (hence the term knots to denote speed at sea) and either a minute glass or a repeated rhyme/song was used which took exactly a minute to recite. The number of knots that passed through the pilot's hand gave him the speed.

Time was kept on board ship in order to measure distance travelled and to set watches (turns of duty by the crew). Sand glasses were the most common method, each glass filling/emptying in half an hour. Bells were rung to mark the half hours – one at noon, two at 12.30, three at 1 and so on until 4 o'clock, when eight bells tolled.

The traverse board was used, however inaccurately, to try to gauge longitude. This was a particular problem for Frobisher because in all three of his voyages he was travelling east–west. The board was a flat piece of wood, usually rectangular with eight holes drilled into it, around a compass face. When the bells tolled the helmsman placed a peg in the board to show the direction of the ship and another to show the speed. After his 4-hour watch, the helmsman took the board to the pilot who would write in the ship's log and mark the ship's position on the chart.

The sounding lead was a means of checking water depth. In harbours and near coasts this was vital and never more so for Frobisher's men because they were often sailing over huge ice-bergs that lay partially submerged and invisible from their ships' decks. It comprised a rope attached to a lead weight that was lowered over the side and had knots tied to it every 6ft (1 fathom in nautical terms). Since this task was carried out by sailors and was an easier task than the more menial work of scrubbing decks and hauling sail, the phrase 'swinging the lead' passed into the language.

Notes

Chapter 1
1. John Chandler, *John Leland's Itinerary: Travels in Tudor England* (Stroud, 1993), p. 46.

Chapter 2
1. William Harrison, *Description of England* (1587), Book II, Chapter 13.
2. Nicholas Breton, *The Goode and the Badde or Descriptions of the Worthies, and Unworthies of this Age* (1616).
3. Thomas Nashe, *Lenten Stuffe containing the Description and first procreation and increase of the town of Great Yarmouth in Norfolk* (1599).
4. Admiralty Report, 1565, lodged at The National Archives, Kew.
5. The Cape was first rounded by Portuguese adventurer Vasco da Gama, 1497–8. Landing on the coast on Christmas Day, he gave the area the name Natal.

Chapter 4
1. Quoted in W.A. Kenyon, *Tokens of Possession: The Northern Voyages of Martin Frobisher* (Toronto, 1975).
2. Quoted in N.M. Penzer (gen. ed.), *The Three Voyages of Martin Frobisher* by G. Best, ed. Vilhjalmur Stefansson (London, 1938).
3. Sir Humphrey Gilbert, *A discourse of a discoverie for a new passage to Cataia* (London, 1576).
4. Quoted in Richard Hakluyt, *The Principall Navigations, Voyages, Traffiques and Discoveries of the English Nation* (1600), p. 39.
5. Ibid., p. 60.
6. Extract from Exchequer records, specifically *Records of the Exchequer, and its related bodies, with those of the Office of First Fruits and Tenths, and the Court of Augmentations*, lodged at The National Archives.
7. Sir John Mandeville, *The Travels of Sir John Mandeville*.

Chapter 5
1. Quoted in Robert Ruby, *Unknown Shore* (New York, 2002), p. 90.
2. Quoted in Kenyon, *Tokens of Possession*, p. 32.
3. Ibid.
4. Robert McGhee, *The Arctic Voyages of Martin Frobisher: An*

Elizabethan Adventure (Montreal, 2001), p. 68.
5. Quoted in Ruby, *Unknown Shore*, p. 90.
6. Ibid., p. 93.
7. Ibid., p. 97.
8. Quoted in Kenyon, *Tokens of Possession*, p. 37.

Chapter 6
1. J.H. Elliott, *The Old World and the New 1492–1650* (London, 1970), p. 7.
2. Dionysus Settle's 'Account of the Second Voyage', quoted in Penzer (gen. ed.), *The Three Voyages of Martin Frobisher* by G. Best, ed. Vilhjalmur Stefansson, p. 12.
3. Ibid.
4. Ibid., p. 13.
5. Ibid., p. 14.
6. Quoted in Penzer (gen. ed.), *The Three Voyages of Martin Frobisher* by G. Best, ed. Vilhjalmur Stefansson, p. 22.
7. Quoted in Kenyon, *Tokens of Possession*, p. 37.
8. Settle's 'Account of the Second Voyage', quoted in Penzer (gen. ed.), *The Three Voyages of Martin Frobisher* by G. Best, ed. Vilhjalmur Stefansson, p. 16.
9. Ibid.
10. Penzer (gen. ed.), *The Three Voyages of Martin Frobisher* by G. Best, ed. Vilhjalmur Stefansson, p. 70.
11. Ibid., p. 17.
12. Settle's 'Account of the Second Voyage', quoted in Penzer (gen. ed.), *The Three Voyages of Martin Frobisher* by G. Best, ed. Vilhjalmur Stefansson, p. 17.
13. Ibid.
14. Ibid.
15. Quoted in Penzer (gen. ed.), *The Three Voyages of Martin Frobisher* by G. Best, ed. Vilhjalmur Stefansson, p. 20.
16. Settle's 'Account of the Second Voyage', quoted in Penzer (gen. ed.), *The Three Voyages of Martin Frobisher* by G. Best, ed. Vilhjalmur Stefansson, p. 18.
17. Settle, quoted in Penzer (gen. ed.), *The Three Voyages of Martin Frobisher* by G. Best, ed. Vilhjalmur Stefansson, p. 18.
18. Ibid., p. 19.
19. Ibid., p. 23.
20. Ibid., p. 24.
21. Ibid., p. 25.

Chapter 7
1. State Papers, Vol. CXXXI, No. 20, Cal, p. 625.
2. Quoted in Penzer (gen. ed.), *The Three Voyages of Martin Frobisher* by G. Best, ed. Vilhjalmur Stefansson, p. 237.
3. Seyers, 'Annals of Bristol collected 1790', quoted in Penzer (gen. ed.), *The Three Voyages of Martin Frobisher* by G. Best, ed. Vilhjalmur Stefansson.
4. Ibid.
5. Ibid.
6. Admiralty reports, lodged at The National Archive.
7. Ibid.
8. Ibid.
9. State Papers, Vol. CXXXI, No. 20, Cal, p. 625.
10. Colonial East Indies, No. 50, Domestic Eliz., Vol. CXIX, No. 41.
11. Eliz. Vol. CXXIII, No. 50, Cal, p. 589.
12. Preface to Thomas Ellis' *A True Report of the Third and Last Voyage into Meta Incognita* (1578).
13. Edward Sellman, *Account of the Third Voyage*, quoted in Penzer (gen. ed.), *The Three Voyages of Martin Frobisher* by G. Best, ed. Vilhjalmur Stefansson, p. 28.
14. Preface to Ellis' *A True Report of the Third and Last Voyage into Meta Incognita*, p. 36.
15. Ibid.
16. Ibid., p. 37. The *Dionyse* refers to the *Dennis*, the name Dennis actually being a form of Dionysus.
17. Ibid., p. 38.
18. Sellman, *Account of the Third Voyage*, quoted in Penzer (gen. ed.), *The Three Voyages of Martin Frobisher* by G. Best, ed. Vilhjalmur Stefansson, pp. 60–1.
19. Ibid.
20. Ibid., pp. 55–6.
21. Preface to Ellis' *A True Report of the Third and Last Voyage into Meta Incognita*, p. 43.
22. Ibid., p. 44.
23. Sellman, *Account of the Third Voyage*, quoted in Penzer (gen. ed.), *The Three Voyages of Martin Frobisher* by G. Best, ed. Vilhjalmur Stefansson, pp. 55–6.
24. Preface to Ellis' *A True Report of the Third and Last Voyage into Meta Incognita*, p. 45.
25. Admiralty reports, lodged at The National Archives.
26. Colonial East Indies, No. 122, Domestic Eliz., Vol. CXXX, No. 17,

'The Abuses of Captain Frobisher against the companie Au 1578'.
27. Ibid.
28. State Papers, Vol. CXXX, No. 17, Cal, p. 621.
29. Colonial East Indies, No. 103, Domestic Eliz., Vol. CXXVI, No. 34.
30. Colonial East Indies, No. 124, Domestic Eliz., Vol. CXXX, No. 18,
   'The Humble Petition of Michael Lok for Charges Disbursed'.
31. State Papers, Vol. CXXX, No. 18, Cal, p. 621.

Chapter 8
1. Elliott, *The Old World and the New*, p. 59.
2. Francis I of France to Charles V of Spain, quoted in William Wood,
   Elizabethan Seadogs. A Chronicle of Drake and His Companions (New
   Haven, CT, 1918), p. 152.
3. Quoted in Wood, *Elizabethan Seadogs*, p. 152.
4. Ibid., p. 164.

Chapter 9
1. Quoted in J.H. Elliot, *Europe Divided 1559–1598* (London, 1968),
   p. 317.
2. Quoted in Garrett Mattingly, *The Defeat of the Spanish Armada*
   (London, 1962), p. 329.
3. Mattingley, *The Defeat of the Spanish Armada*, p. 366.
4. Elliott, *Europe Divided*, p. 332.

Chapter 10
1. Frobisher's will is lodged in the National Maritime Museum Archive.
2. Frobisher's will, National Maritime Museum Archive.
3. 'A discourse of the Queenes Maiesties entertainment in Suffolk and
   Norfolk, etc.' contains the poem 'A Welcome home to Master Martin
   Frobusher' (London, 1578).
4. Thomas Churchyard, quoted in Penzer (gen. ed.), *The Three Voyages
   of Martin Frobisher* by G. Best, ed. Vilhjalmur Stefansson, pp. 230–1.
5. Ibid.
6. Ibid., p. 231.

Chapter 11
1. Charles Hall, *Arctic Researches and Life among the Esquimaux* (New
   York, 1864).

Select Bibliography

Black, Jeremy. *Maps and History; Constructing Images of the Past*, Newhaven, CT and London, 2000

Breton, Nicholas. *The Goode and the Badde or Descriptions of the Worthies, and Unworthies of this Age*, London, 1616

Chandler, John. *John Leland's Itinerary: Travels in Tudor England*, Stroud, 1993

d'Anglure, Bernard (trans.). *Inuit Stories*, Quebec, 2000

Elliott, J.H. *Europe Divided 1559–1598*, London, 1968

Fitzhugh, W. and J. Olin (eds). *Archaeology of the Frobisher Voyages*, La Grange, ILL, 1993

Gilbert, Sir Humphrey. *A discourse of a discoverie for a new passage to Cataia*, London, 1576

Goldsmid, Edmund (ed.). *The Voyages of the English Nation to America before 1600*, Edinburgh, 1889

Harrison, William. *Description of England*, Book II, Chapter 13, 1587

Kenyon, W.A. *Tokens of Possession: The Northern Voyages of Martin Frobisher*, Toronto, 1975

King, J.C.H. *First peoples, First Contacts*, London, 1999

Konstam, Angus. *Tudor Warships (2): Elizabeth I's Navy*, Oxford, 2008

McDermott, J. *Sir Martin Frobisher*, New Haven, CT, 2001

McGhee, Robert. *The Arctic Voyages of Martin Frobisher: An Elizabethan Adventure*, Montreal, 2001

McGhee, Robert. *Ancient People of the Arctic*, Vancouver, 1997

Mattingly, Garrett. *The Defeat of the Spanish Armada*, London, 1959

Nashe, Thomas. *Lenten Stuffe containing the Description and first procreation and increase of the town of Greate Yarmouth in Norfolk*, London, 1599

Penzer, N.M. (gen. ed.). *The Three Voyages of Martin Frobisher* by G. Best, ed. Vilhjalmur Stefansson, London, 1938

Symons, T. (ed.). *Meta Incognita: A Discourse of Discovery: Martin Frobisher's Expeditions 1576–75*, Quebec, 1999

Wilson, John Dover. *Life in Shakespeare's England*, London, 1968

Wood, William. *Elizabethan Seadogs. A Chronicle of Drake and His Companions*, New Haven, CT, 1918

Index